Also by Susie Bright

*Full Exposure: Opening Up to Your Sexual Creativity
and Erotic Expression*

The Sexual State of the Union

The Best American Erotica, 1993–2002 (editor)

Nothing but the Girl (with Jill Posener)

Herotica, Herotica 2, Herotica 3 (editor)

Sexwise

*Susie Bright's Sexual Reality:
A Virtual Sex World Reader*

Susie Sexpert's Lesbian Sex World

All of Susie Bright's titles are available at:
http://www.susiebright.com

How to Write a
Dirty Story
Reading, Writing,
and Publishing
Erotica

Susie Bright

A FIRESIDE BOOK

PUBLISHED BY SIMON & SCHUSTER New York · London · Toronto · Sydney · Singapore

FIRESIDE
Rockefeller Center
1230 Avenue of the Americas
New York, NY 10020

An earlier version of this book was previously published
as *How to Read/Write a Dirty Story.*

FIRESIDE and colophon are registered trademarks
of Simon & Schuster Inc.

For information about special discounts for bulk purchases,
please contact Simon & Schuster Special Sales: 1-800-456-6798
or business@simonandschuster.com

Designed by Chris Welch

Manufactured in the United States of America

1   3   5   7   9   10   8   6   4   2

Library of Congress Cataloging-in-Publication Data

Bright, Susie, 1958–
How to write a dirty story : reading, writing,
and publishing erotica / Susie Bright.
p. cm.
1. Erotic stories—Authorship. I. Title.

PN3377.5.E76 B75 2002
808.3—dc21   2001054809

ISBN 0-7432-2623-2

Acknowledgments

This book was inspired and guided by the words of literally thousands of writers, editors, and readers who've left their mark on me over the years. I'd like to thank my Simon & Schuster editor, Doris Cooper; first draft editor, Bill Bright; and my managers and agents, Joanie Shoemaker and Jo-Lynne Worley. This was my first book that I conceived as both an electronic and print version. My mentors in E-book crime were author M. J. Rose and publisher/author Angela Adair-Hoy at Booklocker.com—thank you for giving me a great start and two excellent role models. I'd also like to thank Richard Hoy, Erika Tsang, Sam Wheeler, Diane Zoi, Andrew Weinstein, Cara Bruce, Adrienne, Jennifer Taillac, Jane Duvall, Ina Nadborny, Aretha Bright, Honey Lee Cottrell, and Jon Bailiff for all their work, support, and encouragement.

Ad Astra Per Aspera

Contents

Contents 9

Part VII. Doing It

Part VIII. Appendix

What You Will Learn About Sex and Writing from This Book

This Is a Practical Book

I **want to** teach you the practice of erotic writing—everything I've learned from twenty years of working with the finest erotic writers, as well as a lifetime of reading the best in sexually inspiring literature. I want to share my knowledge with you as if you walked into my kitchen and we sat up all night discussing every question and investigating every controversy.

In the spirit of making this book work for novices, veterans, critics, and curious bystanders alike, I encourage you to look at the Contents pages and skip around the chapters according to your interests. Get lost in the reader's section, or jump directly into a writing exercise. Discover how writing affects your own sex life, or get cracking on your publishing strategy. Consider this the erotic artist's Scout Manual.

This Is a Mystery Book

Like a good mystery, this book addresses every puzzle, clue, and unpredictable ending you could ask for. I want to help you "solve" not only the dilemma of how to write well but of how to be published well, in order to reach the audience you deserve. Publishing—the "show business" of writing—is a place filled with fears, legends, and fantasies that can bewilder any author.

How we writers reach our readers with our stories seems like a miracle sometimes—because there are so many unwriterly, uncreative obstacles. I've demystified the publishing business for you and given you an honest glimpse of what you can expect, as well as strategies for critical and commercial success.

This Is an Inspirational Book

The most enduring lessons I've learned as an author and editor are how reading and writing affect our sex lives. The reader's erotic world is the place where some of our first fantasies are articulated, where some of our most sensual memories are born. The act of writing for oneself is an unmatched personal experience that goes to the very heart of creativity.

Whether our own stories are published, acclaimed, or paid for—that's a separate concern. Sure, some people will read this book because they want to raise some cash by writing erotica, or they want to create a stir among their friends and colleagues—they'll certainly get a lot of information on how to do that. But this book also has an ethic of devotion to erotic reading and writing as a creative practice, an introspective discipline, and a sexual journey of its own.

This Is a Book of Agitation and Propaganda

I want more people to write frankly about sex. I want to see an end to erotic illiteracy and to the censorship of sexual speech. What other kind of writing can you think of where many people are actually afraid to look at certain words or descriptions on a printed page, or are ashamed to admit they even exist? Can you name ten of the most important authors or books in erotica history—artists whose work turned their world upside down? You will have their names memorized by the time you finish this book. Let's get the stupidity out of so many public discussions that surround sex and art.

This Is a Sex Book

My title, *How to Write a Dirty Story*, is tongue-in-cheek because I don't think anything about sex is "unclean" or unspeakable. I speak candidly about sexuality and the craft of writing in these pages because I want to give you the honest dirt on a subject that is too frequently hidden by shame, ignorance, or elitism.

If any of you garden, you know that you can't grow anything without tending to your soil first. You want the very best dirt for the very best fruit. In that sense, let me offer you an excellent dirty book on a supremely fruitful subject. Enjoy yourself and savor every moment!

Clits up,
Susie Bright

Part I

Thinking About Erotica

How I Ascended:
Becoming an Erotic Goddess

This is the autobiographical chapter of this book: the very quick story of my life in writing. However, you don't need to know anything about me to begin your erotic expression, or to start your reading and publishing adventures. Enjoy my story if you like, or dive into the chapters that address your most important questions today.

I did not have a "reputation" for writing about anything, let alone sex, for the first ten years I was publishing my work. I didn't even know how much I would be affected by my notoriety until I was hit over the head with it.

In 1994, shortly after I began the *Best American Erotica* series, I was interviewed for a cover story by Dwight Garner, a journalist for the *Boston Phoenix* at the time. He wrote that I was the "goddess of American erotica." For the next few hours after I read his glowing praise, I was insufferable. All my sins and weaknesses were washed away as I climbed Mount Olympus with my paper crown.

Later in the day, humbled by real life and toiling in my office, I photocopied the review a dozen times to send to my agent, as well as to publishers I wanted to impress. I thought how curious it was that I had arrived at this place, an erotic "deity." It occurred to me that it had been decades in America since anyone had taken erotica seriously, or treated erotic literature as something to be respected. The trials of the 1950s that made D. H. Lawrence's and Henry Miller's classic works first available legally in the United States were unknown to all but our eldest generation. No wonder I seemed remarkable in my interests and enthusiasm—I was raising a genre from the grave!

I've been asked so many times by fans how, or why, I studied to become an erotic expert. I've been asked which courses I took for my university degree, or how I made my professional calculations to achieve success. The answer is that I did nothing—I mean nothing—to intentionally become a sexpert. Yes, I loved sex—and reading and writing—probably above all other personal pastimes, but without any notion of my affections becoming a career. In retrospect, my progress has been as much a wonder to me as it has been to many of my readers.

I came to sex writing first as a lover, writing poems and letters to my earliest infatuations. Nobody outside my bed knew anything about my erotic devotions.

At the same time, however, I was a political activist; and in addition to the usual suspects, I was also swept up in the early feminist and sexual liberation movements of the 1970s. I started having sex just as the women's movement and gay liberation were peaking. I wrote articles in underground magazines and newspapers about sex, about how to get birth control without your parents' finding out, about coming out gay at your high school, and what to do when you wanted to have a great teenage sex life but you had no privacy and little money—classic themes that I could write about all over again twenty-five years later!

In 1976 I dropped out of high school and became a full-time organizer for a socialist group that was very involved in labor organizing. At the end of the 1970s, my group was split in pieces, and I entered college in southern California to set up camp between the women's studies and theater arts programs. This was the same time that the Moral Majority was founded, when, for the first time in national politics, mainstream politicians raised the issue of the "evil homosexual" as a "lavender" herring.

At this time, although I produced a lot of writing, it rarely appeared with my name on it. The political emphasis at the time was to enhance our collective consciousness and effort. To insist that one needed a byline was considered the worst self-aggrandizing stunt. I would have been embarrassed if anyone had suggested it. I loved the collaboration and the emphasis on group potential; but, in retrospect, I realize that I didn't have any particular sense of my talent for writing. I thought it was just something that everyone needed to know how to do, like cooking for a full house or changing a tire.

To finish college, I moved to northern California, where I found a program at UC Santa Cruz called Community Studies that was devoted to political activism. Best of all, it was largely field study. My major became the pursuit of sexual politics in San Francisco—which at that moment, just after Harvey Milk's assassination, was exploding in several directions.

We were right on the cusp of AIDS and at the beginning of a gay political establishment in San Francisco; instead of merely fighting puritans, gays were now fighting among themselves over who was going to represent sexual diversity in our city's political agenda. Every other sexual minority—from leather folk, to prostitutes, to transgendered men and women—was starting to publish its own books of theory and activism. But the erotic element behind all that protest was still pretty quiet.

I was, and always have been, bisexual; but at that time, every bit of heat in sexual politics was in the gay community. Every straight and kinky person was attracted to the gay scene. It was where every erotic idea was debated and ignited.

I worked a part-time job in a women's vibrator store, composed a play called *Girls Gone Bad*, and read my erotic poetry in abandoned storefronts. It was an exciting time, and it was then that I became frustrated at how little reading matter was available, for women in particular, about our sexual lives and stories. It occurred to me that even though feminism had ignited a revolution in consciousness about women's bodies, we hadn't really gone all the way into a woman's erotic mind.

The Internet hadn't yet become ubiquitous, and as far as books were concerned there was hardly anything—a little Anaïs Nin here, a little Nancy Friday there. Everything erotic in print for women was either antique or was predicated on heavy psychological rationales. Why couldn't women have their own fabulous smut? We were exasperated with much of the male porn that we'd been "making do" with for years.

Two things happened. Joani Blank, the owner of the store where I worked, agreed to publish a book of women's erotica that I would edit—we called it *Herotica*. At the same time, a fan of my poetry readings phoned to ask me if I'd like to contribute to a new magazine for "the adventurous lesbian." It was called *On Our Backs*, and I became its editor.

At that time, no one wrote "women's erotica." It didn't exist as a genre. On the one hand, that made our task of finding talent very difficult, because everyone was so startled by the idea (Women digging sex? Ridiculous!) that it became a challenge to ask any writer to participate. A lot of writers were afraid to use their names, or they wondered if erotic writing would be the end of their careers.

On the other hand, there were lots of women who were writing about sex—beautifully, passionately, and with great intelligence and imagination—and they were shut out of mainstream publishing. I was able to publish authors who, if not for the prejudices of the traditional publishing business, would have been discovered and published to great acclaim.

There was a treasure trove here, and it was being completely ignored. Dorothy Allison, Pat Califia, Sarah Schulman, Lisa Palac, Carol Queen, Joan Nestle—all these great writers who have now been published widely but couldn't have gotten cab fare from a publisher once upon a time. A whole generation of remarkable talent was looking for an "in," and my magazine and anthologies came along at just the right time.

By 1990, after the third volume of *Herotica* and six years of *On Our Backs*, the notion of the sex-positive feminist, with her PC and modem by her side, became ubiquitous. There were dozens of imitators and a flood of talent. Major publishers began to court the new sex-radical divas, and the notion of the "do-me feminist" became a cliché.

In the meantime, I'd become known for my critical and sometimes funny essays about porn, sexual politics, and erotic adventurism. Yet at the same time I was chafing at the boundaries of what I'd created. For one thing, I was bisexual, but most people assumed that I was interested only in lesbian work, since I was so well-known as the editor of *On Our Backs*. Privately, I was appalled that women who dig men didn't have a stronger erotic voice of their own. I was frustrated that I didn't have a venue to publish the work of outstanding gay and straight male writers.

I knew that what erotica fans wanted was something wonderful and new, and they didn't care what the genitals were on the people who wrote it. I knew that the conventional wisdom of the publishing establishment was that gay and lesbian work had to be ghettoized, that straight audiences had to be protected by feeding them only the vanilla fantasies that would fit into their own lives. I'd been looking under people's beds for years, surveying their secret porn collections, and my conclusion was the old maxim: You can't tell a book by its cover.

Right as I was hitting my literary wit's end, I got a phone call. An editor from Macmillan, Mark Chimsky, said he was interested in talking to me because he had heard I knew more about erotic writing than anyone else in America. I'm sure he was soliciting my favor at that point, but his flattery gave me pause. I had never thought of my knowledge that way. I told him yes, it was true—it was a sad commentary on the state of erotica that hardly anyone else cared to become knowledgeable.

I was the "erotica guru" he was after, but it was only because, up to that point, no one else had given a damn. The few scholars who concerned themselves with erotic writing had been isolated and were not involved in the countercultural publishing scene. Most of the prominent mainstream writers of the day were terrified to have their names sullied by "dirty" writing, so they were of no use at all. For me to be the expert, at that point, simply meant that I was a devoted contrarian.

Mark had a concept for an annual series—a collection of the best American erotic writing. The timing was perfect, since I was aching to publish a diverse body of work.

The first edition of *The Best American Erotica*, in 1993, was a national best-seller, and it has continued at that level of popularity ever since. My role has been that of editor and promoter, and also an in-house critic. Each year I've tried to look at the current trends in erotic literature; I've tried to assess what the contents of each volume tell us about sex in America, about writing, about our taboos, and about the status quo. I've written several books of my own that explore my personal sex history and the landscape of American sexual politics.

How did I achieve goddess status? In my more self-deprecating moments, I've said, "Because no one else wanted to." But in a more celebratory mood, I would say it was because of my most elementary passions—sex, reading, and writing—and because my passion for those things became a mission. I was also ambitious at a time when there was a vacuum—where there should have been bountiful literature. There were a lot of beautiful stars in the writing universe to whom no one was paying any attention. I cultivated that world, and it was a galaxy of future Olympians.

Erotic writing today is not only the best work of its kind that we've ever seen in the English language, it also has had an indelible effect on all of American literature. The flinching factor is gone—the former stigma and prejudice against erotic writing have been exposed for the embarrassing ignorance that they represented. If I've acted as a goddess in that stream of events, I've been glad to be part of the faith.

What Is Your Story?

There is no such thing as a person without an erotic story.
I don't mean a tall tale, or a punch line, or a story about the one
who got away.
I'm talking about our personal erotic history, what you might call
our "sexual philosophy."
Take a look at your own erotic story,
and you'll see that it's a motion picture of everything about you that
is creative:
the risks you'd be willing to take,
the weightless depth of your imagination,
your attraction to the truth,
and the things that would make you go blind.

                                        Susie Bright, *Full Exposure*

To begin as an erotic writer (or any kind of writer, for that matter), you need to think you have a story worth telling. You need a certain head of steam that makes you believe your sexual point of view is arousing and fascinating, even profound. You have to think well of your erotic writing talents—sex can make even the most confident of us curl up in a ball of anxiety. Erotic speech is one of the few writing themes that has crippled otherwise self-assured authors.

If you're full of writerly spunk, and just raring to market your latest erotic triumph, then go ahead and skip this chapter—or read it, and perhaps remember when you weren't so bold. But if you are ever plagued with thoughts like "Why am I even bothering to try? Who would ever want to read what I have to say about sex?" then stop here for some relief and reconsideration.

We've been told all our lives that sex is something you perform, furtively, and that you never talk about it, let alone write about it. Even if your family had more liberal attitudes, you couldn't have possibly missed the cultural chill. It's taken a long time to warm up, and only now are we starting to sort out what we have to say about sex. Let's break the ground.

What You Wouldn't Expect About Erotic Writing

• Virgins Can Write Great Erotica

The amount of sex you've had is irrelevant to whether you can observe, describe, and create a potent sex scene. Stop thinking in terms of notches, bouts of intercourse, or orgasm statistics.

Start recording the sexual experience of being alive, noticing what turns you on, listening to how your body responds to your own erotic weather report. After all, what's a bigger turn-on than teenagers' secret diaries of all their lusts and crushes? What's more poignant than a single sexual moment that arrives after a drought? Lack of experience often inspires some of the most excruciating erotic vignettes.

• Really Bad Lovers Can Write Great Erotica

You don't have to be a master at any particular kind of sex in order to write well about it. What you *do* need are empathy and information. You need to care about the issue, not personify it.

Consider how many overweight, chain-smoking, clumsy reporters cover sports with complete devotion. No one asks them if they are great athletes, or if they have even the smallest interest in physical fitness. Likewise, political writers would be the first to admit that they could never be a candidate.

- Really Bad Sex Can Be Great Erotica

The evidence of powerful bad sex can be found all over classics of erotic writing. Often the characters we read about in erotic fiction are inept, cruel, indifferent, manipulative—and yet they can be arousing in their tortured bedroom adventures. A couple of years ago, someone came out with a whole anthology of short stories called *Bad Sex*. Tell me you wouldn't be tempted to pick up such a book if you saw it at your bookstore! There's only one crime in erotic writing, and that's being a bore—the criminal who touches any subject and turns it into lead. A good writer can take even the most seemingly inconsequential act and turn it into a riveting read.

- Erotic Content Can Be Very Small

The pornographic "plain brown wrapper" has served as a misleading role model for a lot of writers interested in sex. In the "porn per page" example, you have to show somebody getting stuffed every 400 words, or else your manuscript is no good. That's an interesting exercise in creative repetition, but it's hardly required, or even desirable.

An erotic scene can be unforgettable, regardless of its length or the number of times such a scene appears in a story. Think of the hottest R-rated movies you've ever seen. Those sex scenes that are embedded in your brain probably took all of three minutes on the screen—a page or two of script at the most. In how many fat novels have you secretly turned down a page or two to mark the erotic highlights? Writing erotica is about quality over quantity.

- Erotic Writing Doesn't Have to Be "Erotica"

The most popular erotic writing today is being done by authors who aren't setting out to write a pornographic tour de force—they just want to include their characters' sexual lives as they would naturally come up in the course of a story. Don't think, "I'm writing an erotica book"; think, "I'm writing a great book, and sexuality will inevitably be part of it."

What's been strange about the history of erotic censorship in America is how often, in a story, the shades are suddenly drawn, an implied act is substituted for an explicit one. But it's as bizarre to eliminate sex from fiction as it would be to exclude any other monumental fact of life. As fascinating and devious as titillation may be, it's been an artificial barrier to more revealing and honest erotic description.

- ## Assume Everyone Is Sexual

This is excellent advice for living, but it's absolutely mandatory advice for writing. If you dwell on stock characters, whose sexual MOs can be spotted a mile away, then you're killing any element of surprise in your plot. You're boring us if you think that, in order to be sexy, your characters have to embody certain physical or psychic measurements.

Mrs. Robinson of *The Graduate* was sexy because she was old and corrupt and unabashedly horny. The Beast in *Beauty and the Beast* was deeply erotic in his desperation and devotion. O in *The Story of O* was an absolutely ordinary little thing whose boundless sexual masochism was in stark contrast to her bourgeois, dull past. Yes, bring on the homely, the deformed, the aged, the plain, and the absurd— these characters are the inspiration for the most profound erotic discoveries.

- ## (Erotic) Writing Requires Ego and Discipline

Once you believe that your writing is worthwhile, that you have something to say, you have cleared the first hurdle. Getting specific ideas is the fun part, because you can use all sorts of inspirations, mental exercises, and outright silly tricks. I've included many of them in this book!

Discipline is hard, by its nature, although such practice is the path to your maturity as an artist. That's how it works—in any genre, for any author. You have to have the ego for writing, and you have to actually do it, rather than dream about doing it, in order to become remarkable. Flourishing as an author is really just another name for showing up and beginning a new page every day.

Is Writing Sex Better than Having Sex?

Sometimes, yes, it is.

Here's the best part about writing sex—once you get started, it's always good. The unhappy part comes when you don't know how to get started, when you hate your first paragraph, when you wonder why you're even trying in the first place.

But once you hit your zone—when the story takes over your mind and you're just taking dictation, when you're laughing at your own jokes and choking up at your own pathos—that's when euphoria, ego, and adrenaline all serve up the perfect orgasmic cocktail.

Writing an erotic scene is arousing, but so is writing any scene you believe is well crafted. You might find yourself writing a brilliant treatise on higher math and find you are unbearably aroused. You might build up a tremendous hunger or exhaustion from writing prolifically. Writing, which is so deceptively illustrated by seated figures scribbling or tapping at the keyboard, is hugely physical, because it demands every bit of your body's mental energy.

Writing sex scenes will make you excruciatingly aware of your body. As you compose your work, you will search your memories to find the most sensitive and lasting observations. You'll remember what you've seen and felt in the most acute way. The strength of your imagination is what makes the fiction come to life; and if you're writing at your best, you're going to internalize those stories—when you're writing them, they feel real.

Writing about sex "works" for writers because, ultimately, it's such a true and vivid part of humanity. The hard part of sex writing is getting to that truth, its most candid expression, instead of the mechanics and morals that we've heard ad nauseum so many times.

The Advantages of Real Sex

The difficult part of "writing sex" is that when you do come out of your reverie, you may be quite alone. I often finish a story with the most blinding desire to show someone what I've done right that minute—and since that's not always possible, I have to face the loneliness that is both the strange comfort and the bane of every writer's existence.

I say "strange comfort" because dedicated writers have a certain taste for their aloneness; while bitter, it's still something we couldn't live without. This is why we often get called "prickly," "oversensitive," "eccentric," and "impossible to live with." This is why every writer takes one look at Virginia Woolf's title *A Room of One's Own* and sighs in recognition.

Many *non*writers who have lots of sex would like to chime in that they too feel just as lonely after their bedroom climaxes, even with their lovers by their sides. I would encourage them to write about that! It's true, though, that body contact alone does not make one feel loved. Still, the traditional forms of sexual relations do provide physical affection and direct arousal, which can ultimately seduce the mind into bliss. With writing, it's the opposite—your craft is always foreplay. You're always getting turned on above the neck first—then later you realize that your whole body is affected.

How About Writing with Someone Else?

Writing as a team, side by side—where you exchange sentences, pages, and concepts, fashioning a work together—is an incredible aphrodisiac. If your results are any good at all, you're going to be attracted to each other. It's competitive, yes, but also thrilling. There's no statistical survey to prove my point, but I defy any writing team to tell me they haven't felt the tug and consequences of the heat they create together.

A (Brief) History of
Sex Writing in America

In the beginning, in America, there was smut. There was no *Best American Erotica* series, because anything erotic was likely to be considered the worst possible taste—if it was considered at all. Like a bastard child whom everyone knows but no one acknowledges, erotica has traditionally had a rich life in American folk culture, humor, and songs—rarely published except surreptitiously, never discussed except in jest or scorn.

I asked my father once, "What was the first 'dirty' story you ever saw?" He recalled that when he was a schoolboy in the 1930s, he came into possession of a page of naughty rhymes, typewritten carbon copies, that were being passed around the playground. This was typical enough—forty years later, I was sneaking my first look at a "fuck book" that was passed through the eighth-grade coat closet. The only thing that changed was the carbon copies. Erotica was simply not printed by any respectable American press, nor sold in ordinary bookstores, until the early 1960s.

American erotic writing lived like this, in a ghetto of prurient interest, until the second half of the twentieth century. It was, and in many places still is, a genre in a segregated twilight world, with many boundaries dictated by class and culture. Until the 1970s, its pleasures and initiatives were largely reserved for men.

The Nature of the Beast

Sexual repression is not simply about words and pictures. Everywhere that erotic art has been suppressed, sexual behavior is similarly curtailed. In any state where laws have prevented adults from consensual relations, there too, the harshest censorship also prevails. In Georgia, for example, not only are you forbidden from performing a cozy act of sodomy in the privacy of your own home, you are also barred from buying or selling pictures of such sinful deeds; you would have to go out of your way even to read about such subjects.

It's not just in the South where we see broad definitions of obscenity; it's all over the United States, in any region where a strong religious tradition prevails over a population that experiences little change.

Our Puritan founders were not known for bringing enlightened erotic beliefs across the Atlantic. More than any other nation that preceded or followed, the United States was founded on a punitive sense of sexuality. That's a remarkable thing to think about. Immigrants, Indians, and slaves who were subsequently conquered/assimilated were each given a walloping dose of Anglo-Saxon-style prudery. The American world of arts and letters came of age under this type of morality and double standard.

When erotica has not been directly banned, it has been derided. It wasn't that long ago that Erica Jong was called a "mammoth pudenda" by the *New Statesman* for her breakthrough book *Fear of Flying*, the first contemporary women's erotic novel. In a different world, I would like to think that such an epithet would be the highest compliment, but in her generation, it was an insult.

Sexual fiction has been ridiculed for lack of intellectual substance or eloquence, and for its commerciality or its dehumanizing qualities. But are these doubts based on our personal feelings about sex? Are we bored by desire, immune to lust, objectified by passion? Hardly.

The bad name given to erotica is a direct result of sexual chauvinism and repression—and their big stick, the legal arm of censorship.

The Early Censorship Wars

The history of literary censorship in the United States is a time line of erotic silence interrupted by fierce but isolated rebellion. When the Bill of Rights was composed, its authors had no clue that the First Amendment would be most sorely tested not by partisan dissent, or abolition, or suffrage, but rather by explicit sexual speech. Think of D. H. Lawrence's *Lady Chatterley's Lover*, first printed in Florence in 1928. Of course, Lawrence was not Italian—his work was considered too sexually explicit to be printed in England or the United States at that time. How about Radclyffe Hall's *Well of Loneliness*, written in the 1920s? It wasn't even erotic, but its mere acknowledgment of lesbianism was considered obscene. In the greatest cause célèbre of obscenity cases, one of our greatest American writers, Henry Miller, did not see his milestone *Tropic of Cancer* available legally in the United States until almost three decades after he published it in Paris in the 1930s.

The Bohemians Come Out

As much as we think of the 1950s as the cradle of American wholesomeness and sexless cheer, those years, in fact, were the dawn of the postwar counterculture—an explosion of poetry, jazz, theater, and political dissidence that, as everyone found out a decade later, turned our world upside down.

In the 1950s, hundreds of American readers passed around underground copies of Miller's soliloquies on the Land of Fuck that he described so vividly in *Tropic of Cancer, Tropic of Capricorn*, and *Black*

Spring. Among those smitten were the heralds of the Beat Generation—William Burroughs, Allen Ginsberg, and Jack Kerouac—and
later, Charles Bukowski. Miller's tradition of declaring the insistence
and prerogative of masculine desire can be seen among erotic writers ever since, even women writers who subverted it for their own
purposes.

The development of erotic writing had suffered for decades from
its stagnation in a quasi-legal atmosphere. Can we imagine what
quality we would find in mystery novels, or sci-fi, if such writing
were banned? When topics are not spoken about, criticized, or appreciated openly, they stay the same; writing about them is reduced
to the habits of shock value and predictable titillation.

The Counterculture's Erotic Renaissance

Music, theater, and film were all revolutionized by the sexual frank-
ness that characterized the 1960s—the first time that the prudish
distinctions between "porn" and "erotica" were strenuously ques-
tioned, and even eliminated. The counterculture integrated its sexual and erotic discussion into its cultural revolution with the motto
The Political Equals the Personal. Feminists analyzed the myth of
the vaginal orgasm, and they urged women to leave the virgin/whore
mentality in the dust. My own generation, which came of age in the
1970s, regarded masturbation as an act of self-determination as well
as pleasure.

While feminists explored the territory of sexual entitlement, gay
male authors, writing for small presses in the 1970s, raised the profound question of sexual identity in literature. Both groups rejected
the notion that diverse sexual expression was necessarily built on a
foundation of guilt and neuroses, but while feminism approached
the topic starting from the viewpoint of theory, the most memorable
gay novels of the same period were first-person erotic memoirs.

The Gay Precedent

Notably, John Rechy wrote eloquently and explicitly about hustling in Grove Press's *Evergreen Review* as early as 1958, when his novel *City of Night* was first serialized. *Evergreen* was exceptional, but Rechy also symbolized a tradition that could be found in Jean Genet, or interpreted through Plato, in which love between men was honored at the same time that it was translated as sexual obsession.

Gay erotic fiction has long been assured of its craft or character, while its heterosexual counterparts have struggled with insecurity and defensiveness. When John Updike, Norman Mailer, and Philip Roth started writing great books with a strong sexual male voice about men and women, it was considered a revolution, but, in fact, this kind of writing had been going on in gay literary circles for ages. To this day, no straight men's sex magazine publishes first-rate erotic fiction, but that is exactly what one could expect to find in reading a popular gay sex magazine like *Drummer*.

One of the most influential and prolific "gay porn" writers and editors, John Preston, made history in 1978 with his erotic leatherman novel, *Mr. Benson.* He published exclusively in pornographic magazines for years, and in the 1990s he initiated one of the classic anthologies of erotica, the *Flesh and the Word* series, in which he (and, after his death, his co-editor, Michael Lowenthal) rescued dozens of amazing gay writers from years of porn obscurity, showing them off in trade paperbacks that reached a "legitimate" bookstore audience for the first time.

The Lesbian Mark

A publisher I met once at a book convention took a look at some of the work I was publishing and said, "I thought 'lesbian sex' was a contradiction in terms!" I doubt he's said that since. The *Herotica* series, *The Best American Erotica*, and even the explicit heterosexual women's romances we see for sale today wouldn't be here if not for the politically incorrect revolution of the 1970s and 1980s in lesbian and women's writing. Lesbians first published their erotic work on their own because they couldn't find a place to publish otherwise. But their audacity, both in word and publishing deed, inspired other women to take their own sexual risks in print.

Pat Califia, one of our most controversial and powerful erotic writers today, was one of the few women ever to have erotic stories featured in gay men's magazines and anthologies. She first wrote about lesbian sex, S/M, and gender-bending when such topics were anathema to the lesbian establishment, let alone anyone else. She is the perfect example of how radical women, and lesbians in particular, transformed the understanding of fantasy, power, and gender roles in erotic publishing.

Califia, whether in her own words or as an inspiration, was central to a lesbian tidal wave of small press books and magazines of the early 1980s, with such telling names as *Coming to Power, On Our Backs, Bad Attitude*, and *Outrageous Women*. Califia's own short story collections, such as *Macho Sluts* or *No Mercy*, convey in their titles the essence of the contemporary radical sex genre: irreverent, confrontational, and unapologetically pornographic.

Fantasy Erotica

Writers like Califia and I were at one end of the women's sex revolution, but it was a different sort of woman writer, married and with best-sellers in her back pocket, who brought homoeroticism onto the best-seller lists. Anne Rice was the first mainstream, best-selling American writer to pen explicit, unapologetic sex novels—*The Claiming of Sleeping Beauty, Beauty's Punishment, Beauty's Release*—

under her own name. Almost single-handedly, she made that kind of cross-genre eroticization popular. Rice delighted in composing the most riveting one-handed reading since *The Story of O*. The *Beauty* series was unabashedly arousing; it transcended boundaries of gender and sexual preference, and the authenticity of its author provided a radical reply to the idea that a woman or a feminist could never write about extremes of sexual desire.

As the originator of the most compelling vampire legend since *Dracula*, Rice not only brought explicit eroticism to her first books about her vampire heroes, she also revealed that her readers—the lovers of fantasy fiction—were an audience ripe for erotic adventure and risk.

The Bloom of Women's Erotica

The pandemonium of the women's erotic renaissance in the 1980s made a lot of critics ask, "Are women more sensitive erotic writers than men?" But women are not naturally more adept at eroticism, and they are certainly less experienced than male authors in charting erotic territory.

It is precisely this lack of background, this "new kid on the block" persona, that made women writers and editors so outspoken. They believed erotica should be displayed and discussed with distinction. After all, women were never included in the deal that men had, in which they enjoyed erotica/pornography privately, away from the family and kids. Men accepted the clandestine third-rate status of sexual entertainment, but women consumers never even had the opportunity to get accustomed to it.

When I first started working in a feminist sex-toy shop, the women customers expected their new vibrators to last like a Maytag. They didn't understand why there weren't shelves of books devoted to women's erotica. I handed them Anaïs Nin's *Delta of Venus* stories from the 1940s: "Sorry, this is *it*." They were appalled, and rightly so. The newly liberated female erotic connoisseur was not content.

The *Vox* of Sex

The first new male author to break with standard masculine conventions regarding straight sex was Nicholson Baker in his novel *Vox*. Its simple premise—a revealing phone sex conversation between two people linked by thousands of optic fibers—constituted the first virtual erotica. Phone sex itself, which has had all the cachet of a knock-knock joke, was transformed in his novel into a most revealing picture of a man and a woman, sharing their souls as they parted their lips.

Baker's departure from the norm is that he portrays the woman character's point of view as convincingly as the man's. Her secrets are delivered on the basis of honest feminine knowledge. The man's vulnerability is entwined with his virility rather than presented as its undoing.

The "Differently Interested"

Of course, readers expect a skilled writer to compose experiences from all walks of life. But in ghettoizing erotica, we have thought that only men could portray male sexuality realistically, and that only women could speak authentically about their desire. Gay and straight sensibilities have been similarly straitjacketed. From Rice to Califia to Baker, a single answer has been given to that tight-fitting cliché: It's over; we've flown the coop.

Popular culture seems inevitably to shake the shoulders of the establishment, saying, "Listen, wake up!" At the same time that erotic work is viewed dimly by the established art world, it manages to make its way under everyone's bedcovers. The hypocrisy becomes unbearable: not only isn't the emperor wearing any clothes, he's also in the middle of an orgy.

Because mainstream publishers were so late to explore sex, a minority of authors bucked the trend of self-censorship and erotic avoidance. It has been the small press and underground periodicals that have mined the treasure of modern erotic writing, and only their successes have inspired the New York publishing houses. Lily Burana, the founding editor of *Taste of Latex* magazine, coined a name for the new sexual material that has changed the bestseller lists: "Entertainment for the Differently Interested." Yes, but there's the point—we *all* have different interests.

The State of the Erotic Union

Erotica has always mirrored politics, reflecting the state of our sexual union and the relative health of our bodies. In the 1990s, AIDS and new practices for safer sex raised tremendous controversy in the sexual entertainment industry. Many people raised "safe sex" visibility as a sort of seat belt directive for erotic artists.

But if writers feel any duty to their work, it must be to deliver both the brutal truth and the most far-flung fantasy. Neither of these has anything to do with including labels and warnings, as if fiction were product advertising. Safer sex practices have inevitably entered erotic fiction, if only because risk itself is an intrinsic part of sexuality. Yet fiction writers will write what's true, not what's on the prescription pad. The panic of lust, the burden of obstacles, and the attraction to denial in sexual relations—those all make for an unbeatable aphrodisiac, and a great story.

When I told a friend that I was editing the very first *Best American Erotica* volume, the first pansexual collection of erotic literature, he laughed at my great seriousness: "Susie, all people want to know is whether they are supposed to get off on it or not."

"Well, of course they are," I said. "It would be a gigantic failure if they read the whole book but didn't find one thing that moved them to a bit of ecstasy."

I didn't like his bottom line. "Listen," I said. "This is a group of writers who aren't content to hold the reader by the balls, or by the tip of their clits. They are people who have something to say about the world, about human nature, about our oldest secrets and greatest mysteries." The mysteries they've uncovered for us, the authenticity of their confessions, are the tracks where erotic writing is taking us tomorrow.

The Similarities Between Erotica and Pornography

Some writers will take one look at the chapter title above and clamp their hands over their ears, or even tear the pages out entirely. Who among the erotic literati can stand another thrash about the true meaning of erotica, as opposed to vital definitions of pornography? For many, it's a debate that has been mired in ignorance and sex phobia from its origins, rendering its arguments absurd from the moment it opens its mouth.

Yet for other writers there's real value in saying that a piece of work is one thing or the other—that in its erotic or pornographic properties, something of value is conveyed to the unprepared consumer. Truly, everything said in the erotic versus pornographic debates is about anticipation: What am I going to get? Am I going to be upset? Am I going to be reassured? If readers were less apprehensive about sex, maybe such advance warnings wouldn't be required.

Let me address those who take an earnest interest in the eros/porn differential. The first thing you have to swallow is this: Even if you embrace the binary categories of porn and erotica, you're going to have to be flexible. It's simply impossible to find any two people who agree straight down the line as to what is in the "E" section and what belongs under "P." Rather than resolving indecision, the best you can hope for is an understanding of connotations, a codebook of clues.

If writers use the word *erotic* to describe their work, they are implying an artistic, educated, and class-conscious element in their compositions. They might be suggesting that women as well as men find the work attractive. They might be making a subtle reference to its more refined or softer qualities. They might be reassuring you that it won't frighten the horses.

Sometimes, if an author says his work is "explicit" erotica, he might be hinting at something that is edgy and frank, yet that has literary ambitions of the highest order. He might be emphasizing that his work is not commercial, or manufactured for purely monetary reasons.

Porn, on the other hand, is a description that is often evoked to produce a more commercial, all-consuming approach. You sometimes hear *Gourmet* magazine referred to as "food porn," which shows how the *porn* word has traveled to other voracious occupations.

Porn often implies the visual—a host of pictures to make you drool. Porn is class-conscious in a different way; it invites one and all, high school dropouts and Ph.D.s, to pull their pants down and drop the pretense. It's often used to exclude women, insinuating that its character is too rough for the ladies. Porn denotes reverse snobbery—it thumbs its nose at erotica for being too weak. The cachet of porn is delivering the quintessential physical reaction.

Still, if you take these definitions literally, you will be lost in the world of sex. You will not understand how these words are shaped and redefined by new users every day.

Just think how far the word *porn* has come in the past twenty years. When I started publishing sex stories, *porn* was a word you just couldn't say at most dinner tables—it had a startling effect. Moreover, porn had changed—from its legal and pathological connotations in the early 1950s and 1960s, to something that was completely redefined by feminists in the 1970s, into a kind of covert operation against womankind itself.

Say "porn" to someone who came of age before women's liberation and that person will probably think pulp novels, *The Story of* O, or Henry Miller's censorship trials. Speak the word to late-era boomers and you'll hear this reply: "Porn equals violence against women." That's quite a leap.

The feminist redefinition of porn was so successful, and it resonated so strongly with the (unfeminist) Christian crusades of the 1980s, that a powerful backlash ensued. Some feminists, particularly the younger generation, started resenting the bogeyman qualities of porn-baiting. They wanted to exalt what their own sexual point of view would look like. In the spirit of punk reinvention, *porn* was reclaimed as a word for exposing subversive, contemporary sexuality.

When I first published *Herotica*, I called myself a feminist pornographer because I knew it sparked such an oxymoronic reaction in many critics. I made a pet out of the *porn* word. It was such a relief to use it for my own purposes, instead of having to hush it and shush it at every opportunity.

The word *erotica* today is the most widely used term to describe all sexual writing and pictures, because it carries the broadest definitions. *Porn* has come to be more defined as pictorial, rather than textual; some people use it exclusively to describe X-rated videos. Porn is often what sex "business" gets called, while no one talks about the "erotica business" because it's too intangible . . . it would be like asking if there were a "philosophy business."

My books use *erotica* in their titles because I want to attract the widest spectrum of readers. I've personally done my part to make the point that erotica is not necessarily sappy, bland, or "for girls only." I'm not the least bit offended by the word *porn;* if anything, I hate the stereotypes and prejudices that get heaped upon it. I like the fact that *porn* has become a more friendly, casual word than *pornography*, which always sounded so terminal.

The lingering problem with the semantic struggles over *erotica* versus *porn* is that they so often are conversation enders, the termination of any kind of dialogue about sex and art. When I talk with someone who wants to get into a labeling argument, I don't want to win the "word war"—I want to change the subject to more intimate terrain. I will entreat my discussion mate to give the definition battle a break. I'll ask something like this: "What do you find sexually arousing to read or look at? What sort of books or pictures turn you on?"

These are the kinds of questions that get to the heart of the matter, because no one is going to quibble over the words *sex* or *arousing*. In response to my questions, my conversation partner either moves to more fertile territory, or else clams up entirely. People with big hassles over the "correct label" are those who can't bring themselves to talk about sex at all. If that becomes clear, then I can reply, "Oh, well, I'd like to talk about sex—when you're ready, let me know."

Actually, I don't know if I've ever been that blunt, but the sulkers get the point. The ball is in their court, and you're no longer on trial to defend your source material as erotic or pornographic.

Sometimes, after you've had a substantive conversation about sex in entertainment or art, you'll return to the erotic versus porn meme. But it won't be loaded with personal defenses anymore. You can deliver your impressions and your sense of humor about the subject without some awful judicial verdict hanging in the balance.

People often ask me when English is going to change—when we'll have words more distinctive and diverse than *erotica* and *porn* to describe the panorama of sexual art. But the English language isn't so much the culprit—it's our puritanical legacy that has dominated our tongue. When people feel free to express something, our language adapts freely and imaginatively. We can then describe our greatest joys, highs, thrills, and amazement—when our sexual stories can live up to all of that, when we decide we want to tell them.

What comes to a woman's mind when she shuts her eyes and thinks about sex? What appeals to the female erotic imagination?

Before we can courageously reveal the correct answer to this question, we have to admit that it's a tough one. Women's sexual expression has been top secret for as long as we've been wondering. It's such a taboo that women themselves don't share, even with each other, what turns them on. To reveal a woman's lust is to admit a sexual power that not everyone is prepared for.

I give the name Femmechismo to the primary signal of the burgeoning women's erotica movement. This is exactly what it sounds like: the aggressive, seductive, and very hungry sexual ego of a woman. Like machismo, it embodies an erotic arrogance; for women, it's clear this is a matter of long overdue pride. Femmechismo has been a well-kept secret. Women have always talked among themselves, in classic pajama party bravado, about their awareness of their sexual power and talent. Sometimes this boasting takes the form of dubious self-effacement. A woman would not typically brag openly about having a big ass in the way a man might boast of his big cock, but she gets her message across by talking about the trials of being an object of such enormous desire.

Femmechismo draws both on a woman's desirability—the excitement she creates simply by being there—and on her sexual talents to influence and make love to her intended subject.

I began my pursuit of women's erotica by looking underneath my girlfriends' beds. Stashed away, but within arm's reach, I discovered back issues of "men's" magazines, Victorian-era ribald short stories, trashy novels with certain pages dog-eared, plain-brown-wrapper stroke books that seemed to have had a previous owner, classics like *The Story of O* or *Emmanuelle,* and even serious critiques of pornography that were paper-clipped so they would fall open to the "good parts."

Women build their erotica collections in a dedicated but haphazard manner. One friend raided her brother's bedroom in the early 1970s for pulp novels with lesbian themes. Another holds on to a ragged copy of *Valley of the Dolls* because it was the first risqué literature she'd ever come across. One plain brown wrapper in my collection came by courtesy of a hitchhiker who left his coat in a friend's car with a copy of *Doris and the Dick* in the front pocket. While many women would never walk into a store to purchase a brandnew copy of *Penthouse,* there are always garage sales, wastebaskets, and back issues from male friends—who might never notice that the May 1978 issue has disappeared forever from their collection.

Feminism opened new opportunities for the female pornographic library. On the blatant side were the feminist erotic pioneers who proudly issued the first volumes of women's sexual points of view. These path-breaking works included Nancy Friday's successful fantasy revelations (*My Secret Garden, Forbidden Flowers*), Betty Dodson's call to self-orgasm (*Liberating Masturbation*), Tee Corinne's explicit *Cunt Coloring Book,* and Anaïs Nin's erotic short stories (*Delta of Venus*). Women finally had a handful of literature that could turn them on. Moreover, they could enthusiastically embrace each author as one of their own.

Another side of the feminist movement in publishing revealed a more devious method for women to discover their prurient interests. If it hadn't been for Kate Millett's tearing apart Henry Miller's sexist prose in *Sexual Politics,* a lot of us might never have been initiated into one-handed reading. As antiporn theoreticians made their case, they cited the most shocking and outrageous examples they could find, apparently disregarding that their audience could be just as easily aroused as offended, and probably would be both.

There's still a lot of confusion about the label "women's erotica." At its worst, it's a commercial term for vapid femininity, a Harlequin Romance with a G-string. However, the very word *erotic* implies superior value, fine art—an aesthetic that elevates the mind, and incidentally stimulates the body. "Women's pornography," on the other hand, is a contradiction in terms for many people; they are convinced that pornography represents the dark, gutter side of lust. We are enmeshed in a semantic struggle for words that will describe our sexual creativity. What turns women on? And why have we been silent on the subject for so long? As we begin to reveal, in detail, the complexity and scope of our sexual desires, the appropriate language will evolve.

At least we can get one thing straight before we wander down the path of feminine hedonism: Some women want the stars, some the sleaze. Some desire the nostalgia of the ordinary, some the punch of the kinky. And some want all of it. Our sexual minds travel everywhere and embrace every emotion. Our sexual fiction is not so different from men's in terms of physical content. Its uniqueness lies in the detail of our physical description, in our vulnerability, and in the often confessional quality of our speech in this new territory.

Porn for Men: The Pitfalls of Formula

Men's sexual literature has been commercialized and compartmentalized into little catalogs of unvarying formulas. In the same way that women have had to "make do" with men's porn, men have had to fit the diversity of their experience into the same pair of tight shoes over and over again. The result is some very stubborn calluses.

Men have made a Faustian bargain: If they agree to keep their erotic interests out of their family life and out of the public eye, then they can enjoy the privilege of varied, no-holds-barred voyeurism. But that variety and that access can only go so far. The embarrassment, the shame, and the double standard that surround men's license to pornography are stifling, and they breed cynicism.

The Feminine Predator

Certainly the stereotype of the female predator is not new—the spider, the manipulator, the schemer. The sex-negative caricature of woman's sexual aggression is that she is evil and that she seeks not an orgasm, but rather destruction and castration. Her scheme of sexual wiles is to procure something other than sex. What's new in women's erotica is that, when women describe their sexual courage and pride, their erotic satisfaction is their explicit goal.

To be sexually adventurous *for her own sake*—not only to feel her own desire, but also to direct it for her ultimate satisfaction—yes, this is Femmechismo. Don't be surprised if its hard little clit comes rubbing up against your leg—purring, of course.

Femmechismo is emphatically not about falling in love, or about "the very first time." It's about the value of a unique sexual experience, desire empowered by action.

When Women Look at Women

Lesbian erotica has been the fastest changing and the most controversial aspect of the renaissance of women's erotica. Lesbian sex stories have been around forever, but they typically were not written by or for lesbians—they were for male fanciers, so to speak, the way a cocker spaniel club might be cultivated. Lesbian stories were typically tales about breaking a taboo, about the sexual possibilities of manlessness. They were more about the men who were not there than they were about the women who were present.

When lesbians began to speak for themselves erotically, it was often in the context of a coming-out story—a woman discovering that she likes women. Self-discovery is the key to the sexual excitement in a coming-out scenario; yet for women of any lesbian experience, one's first sexual encounter with another woman, though an important event, is unlikely to be the most satisfying and revealing experience she'll ever have. The new maturity in recent lesbian erotica is to present lesbian characters who are grown-ups—women who not only desire and love other women but also have the same sophisticated and diverse sexual tastes as anyone.

Radical lesbian sex writers took one of porn's most common questions and turned it upside down: Why do so many men like to watch lesbian sex? The hip lesbian answer is: Because everybody can and does fantasize about anybody and anything they please. A lot of women, lesbian and straight, fantasize about gay men's sexuality, but no one ever made a big deal about it before because no one thought women fantasized about anything except knights in shining armor. The new wave of lesbian erotic writers that grew in the 1980s and 1990s ironically made EveryWoman's fantasy life a lot bigger, because they spoke their minds without worrying about their "virtue."

When a Woman Feels Like a Man

When an ostensibly heterosexual woman writes of her desire for a man, she can also defy traditional roles. It's not at all unusual to find a story in which the woman dominates her male lover, or the man services her. This fantasy has been seen many times, mainly because it's such a popular turn-on for men. In the rare female twist to this role reversal, the woman not only takes control but also takes on a man's feelings and prerogatives, which have less to do with domination and more to do with the masculine world. In the short story "Taking Him on a Sunday Afternoon," from *Herotica 2*, Magenta Michaels describes turning the tables on her husband:

> He clamps up to prevent me from rubbing him there, but aggression has risen in me and I press on, massaging a moistened finger at his entrance. It's slick there and I can imagine the smell, which excites me; I know that he's concerned about the smell, too—how I'll find him—and this excites me even more.

It's the phrase "how I'll find him" that epitomizes the role reversal. Traditionally, it is women who "get found," ladies who worry about what they smell like, and men who relish this vulnerability.

Switching Roles

Sometimes women subvert male sexual excitement by making their own submission almost, but not quite, impossible. They thrive on exuding masculine energy as well as seeking it. It's a Valkyrie demanding her due. In Susan St. Aubin's "This Isn't About Love," another short story from *Herotica 2*, we are introduced to Ilka, a virtual woman warrior—a commando self-defense instructor who revels in her ability to reduce any man to pulp, at the same time as she dreams of a man who could break through her defenses. One dream involves a gun:

> "I was having an orgasm when I woke up," she says. "It was as though the gun that woke me started the orgasm. He finally gave me what I wanted."
> "Death?" I ask. My fingers are clenched under the table. "How can you think you're in love with someone who shoots you?"

"But it was like being shot to life." Ilka looks at me and sighs. "He shot his power into me. I can't explain it, there are not words in any language I know. I'm not talking about love, Chris."

The language that Ilka seeks is not about love—at least not the Valentine's Day greeting card variety, which women have long believed was the greatest literary expectation our passion could reach. Women are approaching a new lover's language today, a roar that comes straight out of our undulating bellies.

Sexual Authenticity

You might be able to fake an orgasm, but you will never be able to fake your way through writing a sex scene. Every reader will know you're a fraud. It's tough that way. No one's going to scold you—they're just going to put your story down and never return to it. Writers are rejected when readers stop reading; they're turned off, and they never come back.

The biggest hurdle as an erotic writer is to write believably. A "good" book never lies emotionally, and a "bad" book always fails because writerly dishonesty is such an inevitable bore. Of course, people make up stories in books all the time; "lying" is part of our profession. But if our "tall tales" are not backed up by emotional truth, if our craft is phony, then the story will never make it out the gate.

Erotica is harder than usual in this regard, because sex is such a touchy subject, and we have to overcome so much cynicism and consumer-oriented titillation. How many books have I read where the story was all fine and dandy until the authors tried to muscle their way into—or sneak on by—a shabby little sex scene? Plenty! Lots of writers freeze up when they come to the sex. It can be shocking to describe what really happens in sexual relations, instead of what is "supposed" to happen or what is "morally" expected.

Ordinary sex, well told, is always an illuminating reading experience. And outrageous sex, described truthfully, will touch the heart of everyone, from the virgin to the Don Juan.

Perhaps some writers don't realize when they're putting the brakes on sex or disassembling their erotic intent. If you're embarrassed about sex, you're bound to avoid it, or you may try to dress it up as something else. If you're determined to make a political point about sexuality, you may find, unhappily, that your sex scenes read like propaganda tracts. In either case, your readers will ignore your shame and skip your agenda, because boredom and disbelief will have already set in. They've put your book down, and you've lost them.

The Truth Test

How do you know if you're keeping it real? To begin with, remember that, in your first draft, your door is closed to intruding eyes—literally as well as figuratively. You want to disappear into the center of your mind's eye, where you can see the sexual scene take place, where you record it faithfully—everything that happens and everything that is felt. You can pretend you're a court reporter or a mystic channeler—you're not controlling these characters, you're just saying what you see and hear.

Let's say you get to a place where the sexual situation demands something you've never actually seen or experienced. Your character has multiple orgasms, or a nervous breakdown, or develops a sadistic streak. Maybe you've had none of those experiences—but you can dig deep into your empathetic wells and climb high onto your mental observation deck so you can imagine those sensations.

I once wrote a story based on a dream I had that Dan Quayle ran away from home to become my besotted lover. It was a very funny story, a satire on Quayle's right-wing politics, but it was also very hot:

You see, Marilyn does not let Danny go down on her. Like maybe she allowed him three times when they were first together, and then it came to a complete halt. Of course, he is just cunt-mad. He buries his head in my fur and simply will not come out—my orgasm is just one curve in the coaster to him. He sucks the cum out of me, licking me like a bowl of chocolate, holding my clit hostage. The only way I can bring him up to eye level is to beg him to fuck me.

And, geez Louise, his cock is such heaven. I mean, what are the qualifications for a great fuck? Spelling ain't one of 'em. Neither is any kind of brains, let alone progressive politics. Like so many other cruelly teased bimbos, Danny is, bottom line, a very physical and sensual animal who is at his happiest driving balls into holes. The man is an athlete, an Olympian.

For one, he just won't come until I do, long after I do, and then he only pauses to cradle me for a moment and ask if I'm not too sore to carry on. And thanks to a 16-ounce bottle of lubricant, I am not in a wheelchair as we speak. His cock is not the biggest dick in America, but it is definitely something to show off.

Of course he's cut, and his erection flies straight up, not curving or bowing. The head looks like a polished marble doorknob, only to touch it, of course, it's like purple velvet. In fact, his hard-on turns rosy violet the longer he moves in and out of me. His cock is so pretty that I apologized to him that I was not adept enough to take it all down my throat—I've never been great at that—but he just looked at me like I was crazy and whispered, "Just lick me, baby."

He loves me to tongue the underside of his dick, from the bottom where his balls sit cuddled in anticipation, lapping right up to the cleft in his cock-head. When I suck him this way, he starts whimpering and, needless to say—no, I'll say it again—he crawls inside my pussy once more with his mouth as hungry as a girl's.

Now, obviously I have no idea what Dan Quayle's personal sexuality is like. But this passage rings true because:

1. The physical sex descriptions are based on a real-life lover.
2. I know perfectly well what it's like when opposites attract.

3. I had Quayle's official bio down cold, and I was very familiar with the drubbing he'd taken among America's intelligentsia.
4. I could describe how very masculine men could become feminine and needy in bed.

My story had an outrageous air of believability about it because of its *plausibility*. All its elements were honest.

I don't think writers are necessarily the most honest people on earth, beyond the writing desk. We screw up and fib and con like anyone else. But when we write, we have to give all that up for the words. The words don't work when you fail to make them plausible. Our job is to suspend disbelief.

To be an honest writer, you don't have to adopt the ethics of right livelihood. Go ahead, be a scoundrel and a phony in your real life. Just know that you're not going to be able to keep that up when you're writing, unless it's for your own hypnosis.

Sexual authenticity in writing is best cultivated by reading—reading great erotic authors and stories, and being inspired by them. You'll have the startling pause of recognition, you'll see passages of intimacy that you didn't know could be captured in words. You'll be aroused as if you were in the middle of making love. Find the stories that move you, and make them your role models.

The afterglow of creative sexual authenticity is that it gracefully becomes the standard for all your writing destinations. With all the credibility you bring to erotica, you'll find the writing wisdom that touches any important part of a life story.

When you're ready to edit your work, hold the sex scenes up to your highest scrutiny. Pretend they're death scenes, pretend they're the crux of your plot, pretend that this is the first page. They may very well be all those things. How well do they hold up to the pressure? If you can conclude, "This is as good as or better than anything I've written," then you've nailed it—now you can start comparing your other writing to your erotica!

Writing Erotica for an Audience of One

Writing about sex for yourself, or to share with a lover or dear friend, is the quintessential reason to write erotica at all.

Sure, the hype is that erotic writers do it for money, notoriety, rebellion—but truly, the most profound and persistent sexual writing happens because people want to articulate their desires in a way that, first and foremost, amazes themselves. You get off on it—that's the criterion. That experience could be entirely mental, or it might leave you in a wet puddle, but the catharsis is yours alone.

Why do we keep diaries, write love letters, or scribble a story and keep it in a special place that we can return to again and again? When we write an experience, we relive its sensations and see it from different angles. Writing takes memories and turns them into virtual reality. Long before computers ever came along, this is what writing did for us—it transported us.

I have a writing exercise for my erotica classes in which I ask them to write the story of the *last* sexual experience they had before walking into my classroom that day.

It's quite challenging—I let them define what "sexual experience" means on their own terms. I'm not looking necessarily for the last act of intercourse, or even the last orgasm. Nevertheless, the assignment is provocative, because the "last sex" you had is not necessarily the stuff you want to brag about—maybe it was ordinary, maybe it was painful.

In each case, when my students turn in their work to me, they comment that regardless of whether they were writing about a good time or a bad time, about something that happened an hour ago or a year before, the concentration it took to write it was like "reliving it all over again." They felt the heat, the anticipation, the ambivalence—all of it.

My reply was that if they felt that way, the writing had been successful—I could give them an A right then without reading it. They had accessed the muse that everyone loves dreaming about.

On the other hand, if I have students who say they couldn't think of anything, or it was too "boring" to bother writing down, or they've only scribbled down a couple of words as if they were entries on a calendar ("Fucked Jane at 11 A.M. before work")—I know they've avoided the central question. They don't want to relive their last sexual experience; their dread of those memories is just as distinct as the connectedness of the students who threw themselves into theirs. But until they go there, wherever "there" is, they're not getting anywhere with their erotic writing.

Your authentic sexual expression is a prerequisite for erotic publishing. If you can't get that far, you're never going to write successfully for the masses. But the opposite is *not* true: You don't need to publish in order to write well, and writing well for oneself is perhaps the sweetest thing of all. In personal writing, editing is not the point, let alone packaging and marketing. You become articulate to yourself, you compose your own sexual philosophy, and your writing practice is your divining rod.

When I began writing, of course, it was largely for myself. I've enjoyed going back to some of those stories and poems, filed away in my drawers and scrapbooks, to take a look at what my thoughts were in those days. Sometimes, the publisher in me thinks, "Oh, that's not half bad, I should rewrite this for publication."

But what I really think about my old poems and diary entries is that they are quite perfect the way they are. They reveal my vision and passion at the time they were composed; they make me shake my head in wonder.

Having given so much of my writing time over to my professional career, I envy those days when I was so impulsive, when I gave in to every emotional display. I can barely write in my diary anymore without feeling a ghost editor commenting over my shoulders. I'll even yell at myself, "Shut up, *Esquire* isn't reading this! *Ms.* magazine doesn't care! This is not a *Rolling Stone* interview!"

Professional writers need personal writing to remember who they are, away from the critics and the crowd. Solo writers, who write for their own private benefit, have the key to open that secret garden anytime they want. They may be perfectly and justifiably satisfied to keep it all to themselves.

Part II

Reading It

What Do You Like . . . and Where Do You Find It?

Erotica must be the only writing genre in the world that people think it's fair to critique even if they've never laid eyes on it. You can walk into any literary workshop or classroom in America and boldly announce, "Erotic fiction is complete rubbish"—no one is likely to question your credentials or background in the subject.

Erotica is plagued by critics who call it foolish and trivial. What they don't realize is that such comments say a whole lot about *them* —as individuals who are poorly read and sexually ignorant—but very little about the literary genres or giants of erotic writing.

No one who has read much of Henry Miller would have the nerve to say that the best literature cannot be sexual. No lover who has memorized whole passages of *The Story of* O can say that erotica hasn't made an impact on millions.

To write erotica, you need to read it, and you need to take some inspiration from the history of some of the world's writing geniuses. If you love Mark Twain, you must read his bawdy *Diaries of Adam and Eve*. If you have been schooled in James Joyce, you must consider his erotic muse, Molly Bloom. Few have matched his prose when it comes to a man's state of mind inside his lover's cunt—and yes, that's what he would call it.

One can read about sex with a mechanical approach, searching for a new twist to add to your sexual repertoire, a fresh titillation for your fantasy bank. There are many who treat erotica like cookbooks, searching for new recipes. To a certain extent, that kind of discovery is inevitable—just as you might read a novel set in Morocco and decide that you must travel there next week. Sometimes erotica is going to inspire direct imitation.

But more often, erotica is not read like a manual; it's not an exercise video. It's often about characters and situations we could never experience in real life but that exercise powerful effects on our imagination.

The more you read and pay attention to erotica, the more you will become fascinated with its psychological depth in the hands of masterful writers. You will be in awe of the talent it takes to evoke the intimacy of even the one-night stand.

I suppose I began my education in erotica through sheer attraction to the taboo of it. As a child, I knew that books like *Lady Chatterley's Lover* were supposed to be naughty; I heard grown-up discussion about how it had been banned. When Erica Jong's *Fear of Flying* came out, I read the reviews that called it scandalous—shocking, "for a woman." Gossip about books like this piqued my curiosity and had me looking for such titles on every bookshelf. I had no idea what was supposed to be "trash" versus high art, so I was just as thrilled and curious to find *The Sensuous Woman* on my aunt's bookshelf as I was to find my mother's copy of D. H. Lawrence in an old army trunk. I sneaked peeks at copies of *The Happy Hooker* that were being passed around my sixth-grade classroom.

Of course, as soon as I began actually reading these books, I noticed the differences right away. A bunch of torrid confessional letters to *Penthouse* could be skimmed very quickly; I was intensely aroused by some letters but laughed at others. I got hold of John Updike's *Couples* because I read in some women's magazine that it was "steamy," but then I became so engrossed in his voice that I read every other Updike book in print that summer. Because of Updike, Jong, and Lawrence, I now took it for granted that the most honored writers in print were just as likely to write great erotica as anyone.

I was also an ardent teenage feminist. I wanted to find women who wrote about sex who would let me share their clit-lit point of view. At that time, all female erotic roads led to Anaïs Nin, and she was a revelation in that regard. I couldn't believe that a woman would write so candidly and exquisitely about sex in the 1930s—yet there didn't appear to be anyone like her in my generation.

My search for erotica, and my trial-and-error approach to finding what I liked, was hardly efficient. I sought out what was "banned," then I'd occasionally find one author I liked and read everything he or she ever wrote.

At that time there were no cheat sheets or expert lists on what should be stocked in an erotic reader's must-have collection. The one time I found a history of erotica, it listed nothing but British Victorian spanking classics; while I was delighted to find out about those as well, they hardly gave a complete picture.

Today, with so much contemporary erotic fiction out in the open, you can probably accomplish in a few months what took me years. You can focus your efforts on one particular genre—British lesbian gothic, for example—and find a gold mine.

But if you're a beginner, as an erotic reader or writer, you will do best to familiarize yourself with several kinds of erotic storytellers. You should articulate in your own mind who you like best, and why. Whatever your own original style is, it will only be sharpened by understanding who's come before you and how the erotic genre has developed.

"WHAT DO YOU LIKE?" EXERCISES

I don't think there's anyone who longs to write who doesn't already love to read. But some writers feel that overreading will damage their writing process. Their fear of influence is misplaced. Reading works that you like will inspire you to write more, and it will improve your craft. Reading erotica, both the laudable and the laughed at, will give you the versatility and insight that you need to tackle erotic depth.

PART I

What You'll Need: *Some uninterrupted time to read*

Familiarize yourself with novels or short stories from the following erotic genres. I've listed a well-known author or title in each genre if you don't already have a favorite yourself—these are hardly the only ones, just a few standard-bearers.

Erotic Romance	Robin Schone's *The Lady's Tutor*, Rosemary Rogers's *Sweet Savage Love*
Erotic Sci-fi	Cecilia Tan, anything from Circlet Press, *Crash*
Gothic	Anne Rice writing as A. N. Roquelaure
Horror	Lucy Taylor, Poppy Z. Brite
Plain Brown Wrapper	Anything by Anonymous, *Penthouse Letters*
Victorian	*The Pearl, A Man and a Maid*
Women's Erotica	*Herotica, Fear of Flying, Delta of Venus*
Modern Classics	Henry Miller, *Lady Chatterley's Lover*
***The* Classic**	*The Story of* O
Mystery/Thriller	*In the Cut*, the *Noirotica* series
Lesbian	Pat Califia, Tristan Taormino, *Hot and Bothered*
Gay	John Preston, John Rechy, *Flesh and the Word*, Aaron Travis

PART II

What You'll Need: Writing paper, a pen, scraps of paper or index cards, a kitchen timer you can set quickly for three minutes.

- Write down the genre names that you feel familiar with (from the above list) on separate slips of paper. Put them facedown, shuffle, and choose one.
- Set the timer to three minutes and begin writing in the most blatantly sexual, clichéd imitation of this genre you can muster. Be completely uninhibited; don't try for finesse, just use broad strokes.
- If you can't think of a first sentence, take this line and begin: "S/he reached for the door and . . ."
- When your alarm rings, stop writing on the spot.
- Draw a line under your first passage and set the timer again for three minutes. Choose another scrap of paper.
- Continue writing the story you've begun, only in this new genre. Don't worry about changing the scene, time, or any other illogical leaps; just get busy with this new interpretation of the action.
- Change genres every three minutes in this fashion until you've come to the end of your scrap pile.
- Read your entire, fractured-genre story aloud. If you have a group or partner to share this exercise with, so much the merrier. Of course, it will be funny to hear your stabs at these different styles, but your laughter will be instructive.
- Answer these questions: Which genres were the easiest for you to imitate? Is that because you like to read those genres the best or because you find them the simplest to satirize? What clichés are the icons of these various writing traditions? Do you ever see their influence in your own writing? Which style was the hardest for you to riff on? What does that tell you about your own writing?

Goal
- Increase your knowledge of the variety of erotic writing.
- Learn from the masters of the craft.
- Find out which styles you've been most influenced by.
- Sharpen your own writing style by having some fun with others'.

After You Finish This Exercise, You'll Never Believe Again . . .
- That erotic writing is all alike.
- That writing "dirty" is a snap.
- That your writing has been unaffected by the erotic classics.

The first time I tried this exercise, I found that anything with a female viewpoint was easier for me to approach. However, I was surprised that the "Erotic Romance" caricature came so easily to me, because at that time, I wouldn't read those kind of books—I was embarrassed by them.

But after my writing exercise, I realized that I had read so many of these books as a young girl that the formula was hardwired in my brain. I also saw that what appealed to me about romance books was that they are unapologetically romantic. The power dynamic between a dominant and a submissive proves an irresistible way to drive forward any plot. Both these elements were styles of writing I wanted to master.

No matter how low or high a genre might be classified on the literary marketplace, it has something vital about it, and it can teach you something as a writer. Before you toss a "Plain Brown Wrapper" in the trash, ask yourself: Why does anyone get off to this? What do these authors know about pushing buttons that take readers out of their workaday orbit? Someday you'll want to write a piece of dialogue as visceral as any smut peddler's, and you'll want to know: How do they do that?

You might find some genres elusive to imitate because you don't know the style well. But when you try your hand at imitating a "literary masterpiece," what are the details or aspects that you're aiming for?

These "imitation" writing exercises are not designed to destroy your own originality—quite the opposite. This is like learning a new dance or a new language—your whole sensual vocabulary and empathy are going to open up when you get a taste of how other writers find their erotic nut. When you go back to your own writing, you'll feel a repertoire available to you that you didn't feel aware of before. These exercises are taking the natural impulses of a bookworm—to drink up the essence of many writers—and take it into your own self-expression.

If you find yourself completely blanking at one of the genres I've listed, it's because you haven't read enough of it. You can't create a stereotype, or a quick pass at a genre, if you don't know your subject well. Back to your reading couch you go!

The Good Parts

When I was thirteen, I moved from California to Edmonton, Alberta, where it snows from the first of September to the end of May. I had never seen snow fall before I moved to Canada, and it had never occurred to me how a change of climate would change every aspect of my life.

Take school, for instance: Each class had a sizable cloakroom, where thirty kids could remove their down jackets, backpacks, and snow boots before the bell rang. The cloakroom was warm—overheated, in fact—but it was also dimly lit. It was the one place in the school where all of us were together without adult supervision, and the few minutes when we congregated there before the bell rang were the most intimate and clandestine of the day. Subjects under discussion were routine: sex, cigarettes, and hockey bets. The boys would try to get a rise out of us girls by messing with our things, and we rose, squealing, to the occasion. In the thick of it, we smelled like dirty snow and gym socks.

The most popular girls, the toughest ones, were into trading books and smokes. One day Barb Janssen, who wouldn't normally talk to me, passed me a paperback copy of Mario Puzo's *The Godfather*. I'd never seen the title or author before.

It was the first time I was ever handed a book and told, "This is dirty." I was also given a footnote: "Check out page 27," Barb said, pulling the book out from beneath her sweater. I felt myself blush, just hearing her say the number under her breath.

I wouldn't read it in front of her—I was afraid I wouldn't understand the "dirty" part, that it would somehow pass me right by, like most of the jokes that got the biggest snickers in the cloakroom. I was a dweeb, and by the look of this book's dog-eared cover, I must have been the last person in class to get a crack at it. I knew that if I could only be alone with it, I could take the time to look up every word and get to the bottom of the dirtiness. With *The Godfather* to help me, I could get rid of my virginal reputation.

At lunchtime we were allowed two hours to go home for our meal and trudge back across the snow. I knew my mom wouldn't be home and I'd have the apartment to myself, just me and page 27.

As an impatient book lover, I certainly had sneaked peeks at the last pages of novels before, but I'd never turned to a paragraph in the middle of a book to begin my read. I didn't see the point in starting at the beginning of the novel, though; Barb said it was a dirty book, and that meant that it was only useful for one thing, the "good part."

The magic page fell open before me—the binding was broken there, of course. I began to read:

[Lucy] felt something burning pass between her thighs. She let her right hand drop from his neck and reached down to guide him. Her hand closed around an enormous, blood-gorged pole of a muscle. It pulsated in her hand like an animal and almost weeping with grateful ecstasy she pointed it into her own wet turgid flesh. The thrust of its entering, the unbelievable pleasure made her gasp, brought her legs up almost around his neck, and then like a quiver, her body received the savage arrows of his lightning-like thrusts; innumerable, torturing; arching her pelvis higher and higher until for the first time in her life she reached a shattering climax, felt his hardness break and then the crawly flood of semen over her thighs.

This was the first time I had ever been exposed to the "big cock" meme. I was so sheltered, I had no idea that bigger was supposed to be better, or even that penises came in different sizes. I found this enormously titillating. Did vaginas come in different shapes as well? What size was mine? Did I have any say in the matter? What if you ended up like Lucy? If you couldn't find a Sonny penis, were you doomed to never have an orgasm?

I didn't know the first thing about intercourse, but the appearance of those salacious words filled me with fear, guilt, and—though I couldn't have articulated it at the time—erotic anticipation. Feeling hot and feeling scared are remarkably similar sensations. I imagined what would happen if my mother came home and saw me reading this filth on the ironing board. Or what if the book fell out of my backpack on the way to school? It had a magenta cover, and everyone in Edmonton would see it there, like a bloodstain on the ice.

While I ate my sandwich, I read the "good part" over and over. With additional readings, it wasn't quite so drop-dead exciting. I started to wonder who this Sonny was anyway, and what was going to happened to him if he missed the wedding party. I turned to the first page of the book, and began reading from the top.

I was fifteen minutes tardy for our postlunch class period. Mr. Johnson, my math teacher, gave me the withering look that he saved for Americans. I sat down in front of Barb, who pinched my arm from behind.

"Where is it?" she hissed. "Did you read the good part?"

"Yeah," I said. "But you know, the whole book is really good; I'm way past page 27 now."

Barb's jaw dropped so far I could see everything she ate for lunch still stuck in her braces.

"You're reading the whole book? You are such a moron!" Dropping my sleeve, she left her seat, eyeballs rolling, to rendezvous at the pencil sharpener with Sharisse and Sandy, the reigning cig queens of the cloakroom. I couldn't look at them; my stomach was in knots. I'd thought it would be cool to read past page 27—and in fact, it was irresistible. Now I was screwed; I was never going to hear the end of it, and all because I didn't know that dirty books weren't for reading.

But I had made an important discovery—one that wouldn't help my social status but helped me a lot in my future writing career. Puzo's novel had more than one good part, but each "part" got all its oomph if you knew who the characters were and could see how the sex part set them up for the next turn of events. Sure, on a first reading the forbidden words gave me a thrill, but I could only squeeze the juice out of that for so long. By the end of the novel, I was no longer a girl who was going to be startled at the sound of the word *vulva*.

Any adolescent virgin will get a kick out of reading naughty bits on a page, and so will those who've been told that Satan will spirit them away if they're caught with such filth. But skilled writers can't rely on juvenile and repressed readers to carry the erotic weight of their novels—they have to create a wonderful whole to support each erotic scene.

You can't create the zing of a steamy episode without stringing your harp good and tight to begin with. This is why the mechanics of character, plot, and timing are essential for even the smallest sex scene to make its mark.

Many writers don't want to write "erotica" per se, but they nevertheless want to include a small amount of erotic action in their stories. Such writers can't assume that erotic scenes will be simple, or divorced from the pace and motivation of the rest of their character's actions.

You need to know how your protagonists sleep, eat, dream, and bleed before you can throw them into a sex scene. You don't have to spell out every detail of the back story to the reader, but as an author, you have to know it. Writers who think they can lay naked bodies down on a bed, throw in a few moans and groans and be done with it, are going to find their characters are wooden and unbelievable.

I once was on a panel of filmmakers who were being interviewed about how they shot a love scene. None of these directors was comfortable with the subject, and one of them quipped out his strategy: "I try to leave the room." When I considered his current movie, I could see he wasn't joking! I was appalled to see that his colleagues were shaking their heads in amused sympathy.

You can't leave the room if you're making a movie, and you can't leave the room when you're writing the script, either—not if you want anyone to respect your results. Every time creators cop out on a scene, and relegate it to some kind of unwanted but mandated prop, they're losing their credibility.

What if you're not burdened with these ambitions? What if you want to write a wall-to-wall smut fest? You can have your lovers out of their panties and writhing on the floor in the first paragraph. But if you don't set up some basic conflict, or the platform of character development, then you aren't going to hold the attention of anyone except a censor looking for dirty words with a red pen. That's why, even among the cheapest "Plain Brown Wrappers," the stories that sell the best are the ones that remain most faithful to a traditional narrative.

Think about comic books as an analogy. Comics are another genre where the writing has been disparaged; supposedly it's all just "Wham, bam, thank-you-masked-man." Yet the most popular comics are those in which the readers feel powerfully attached to the superhero and villain—where the suspense and thrill of what's going to happen next never fails to disappoint. As comics have matured over the decades, the most popular heroes have been those who had doubts and vulnerabilities in addition to their amazing strength.

There's a craft to writing a love scene or a sex scene—in that you're focusing on a physical description that you want to come alive, as well as an interior description of how the sex feels. But these scenes will come across gracefully only if you know why your bed partners are together in the first place, or why your masturbator ends up alone with his dick in his hand. Give your players a life and a challenge to overcome; then their sex life will take its cues from their circumstances. Don't think, "sex scene = plot recess"; think, "sex scene = plot engine."

In *The Godfather*, the eldest son's recklessness, his ego, and his defiance of his father are all superbly set up before he plows the bridesmaid. His sex drive is one of the things that attracts us to him, but it also makes us anticipate his downfall. It certainly was a "good part," but it was good because it stimulated not only our libidos but also our attachment to Sonny's future. Puzo arouses his readers' senses, whether through erotic fascination, or horror at the brutality, or even through our appetite to taste the meals that accompany every part of this Italian family's rituals.

Write the good parts, fine, but before you get to your juicy climax, write *all* the parts—in your mind, if not on paper. Sexuality is not a spice that you add after the meal is done. It's the oil that you start cooking with, and that's a flavor you don't want to forget.

Reading Aloud

Two traditions of reading aloud are still thriving in America today. One is reading children's stories to the very young—*Winnie-the-Pooh*, *Goodnight Moon*, and, now, the adventures of Harry Potter. The other time we commonly read aloud, speaking verse or prose, is when, as lovers, we read to each other in the spirit of seduction.

What both these story hours have in common is that they're bedtime stories—the tales told before falling into dreams, or into each other's arms. I've often wanted to do a survey of how many people have shared their favorite erotic passage with someone they desired or wanted to impress. I know that each year, when I publish *The Best American Erotica*, I hear from fans who want to tell me about a particular story that they read to their lovers.

It's the tradition of Scheherazade. An erotic story is a yarn that we will crave night after night, crafted into one seductive knot after another. As someone who loves to be read to, I know what the impatient sultan must have gone through for lack of a good story. I, too, have often been so upset when a favorite book came to an end that I've threatened to chop my storyteller's head off if he or she couldn't come up with something else to compel my attention.

When I was a child, in the Catholic schools that I attended, there was still a tradition that all students should memorize lengthy prayers, a rosary strand of recitation. We also were given assignments to memorize long poems by Tennyson and Longfellow. My fifth-grade teacher, Mrs. Henning, stipulated that every poem we chose to recite must have at least one hundred lines. I was delighted to choose Lewis Carroll's "The Walrus and the Carpenter" for my spring effort, but Mrs. Henning gave me a D because she said the content was the stuff of "amateur theatricals."

Mrs. Henning had my number: I loved everything about theater, high and low. Onstage, both as a child and an adult, I found the opportunity to indulge in all sorts of delicious verse and dialogue. It not only improved my memory, but also my delivery and my aural charisma. When I published the first editions of *Herotica* and *The Best American Erotica*, my first notion of how to promote the books to the public was to schedule a spoken-word performance.

For writers who love to show off, this voicing of erotica is pure pleasure. But for those who are shy, it might not be obvious that the essential nature of erotica is to be spoken aloud.

You may never perform your erotic prose aloud; you may never appear onstage or at a mike. But if your erotic work is successful at all, it will be voiced by your readers. This is a litmus test for erotic speech. You must not only write your erotic story in order to create it, you must also *hear* it. If your lips are pasted shut in apprehension, you're going to have to find a volunteer.

Reading one's work aloud is the first step writers and editors take to bring a work out of the unconscious and into the light. I've always been convinced that the reason that electronic-product manuals are so often incomprehensible is because, with no literary tradition to guide them, the publishers have never read these works aloud. If any of the VCR companies had bothered to read aloud the user's manual for their machines, they would see that it makes no sense in any of the five languages they offer.

I've never published a word that I didn't read out loud before I put it to bed. That's the quickest way for me to see where the pace is falling apart, or where the sentences are turning into Greek, or where the tone is going all wrong. If you're ready for a real tonic of objectivity, you can even tape yourself reading your work, and then play it back. Active listening to your work is yet another degree of audience point of view and separation.

Whether you become a complete vocal narcissist or you shyly ask a trusted friend to read your work aloud, you must include this experience as an erotic artist. I would say the same thing to poets and to writers of children's fairy tales. Your material is meant to be heard.

When you do read erotica a aloud, there may be the moment where you clutch and say, "I can't say *that*—out loud." I've been surprised by some of my favorite authors who couldn't say the "dirty words" in their own stories. My friend Michelle Tea—whose hair is frequently blue and who writes entire novels about working as a hooker and living in various lesbian colonies—turned five shades of red when she was asked to read her latest erotic story, "10 Seconds to Love," to a circle of fellow authors. She hung her blue head down to her chest, and whispered:

> Tommy's cock was huge, he rubbed it with one hand while the other probed my pussy, separating my lips and fingering my hole. My little cunt felt huge, all swollen and wet, and he brought the tip of his cock down to it and started nudging . . .

I had a hard time not channeling my old fifth-grade teacher, Mrs. Henning, demanding that Michelle stand up straight and e-nun-ci-ate before I had to get out my ruler.

Still, witnessing a gifted author bite her lips over her own erotic confection is powerful evidence of how just the utterance of a few dirty words can make more than the audience tremble.

Some of my funniest and earliest experiences of reading erotica aloud happened when I was a teenager, going to Venice Beach every summer day with my girlfriends. We would spread out a flotilla of towels, roll a joint or two, open the pizza box, and read to each other from pulp novels.

"*Take* me, Fa-bio." I'd recite. "*Thrust* your purrr-ple hot spear into my *aching* pink love canal!" We'd breathlessly emphasize every other word until, through a combination of hyperventilation and helpless laugher, the book would fall from our hands, or be grabbed by the next eager orator. We didn't just stop at the purple prose, either; we'd gamely move on to more blunt readings of the "hard-core stuff." I think those summer days were the first times I ever said "bad words" aloud—for effect, to an audience. It was a great reliever of our teenage sexual tension, and it also helped us think about how phony and forced this kind of language can be when it is overcome by cliché.

For the writer, using taboo words and sexual slang is like using the dynamite in your kit. You need to be judicious for maximum impact, realizing that a little goes a long way. If your character is saying "Fuck me. Fuck this" in every other line, you might have a colorful character on your hands, one whose conversations reveal a great deal about his condition, but you will have lost the shock value of the "f-word" for any erotic purpose. That strategy could work if you are clever, because when you come to that character's sex scene, you'll have to come up with something else to show us how affected he is by his erotic transcendence.

Pay attention to how "swear words" pack a wallop, or how they can fix your character in the reader's mind. It's a good lesson in seeing how all the words you use are bullets, each with its own particular impact. Writing them down affects us, as the originators; and saying them aloud unleashes them into a reality that they won't achieve silently in our minds.

EROTIC READING EXERCISE

How do you begin to read erotica aloud, if you're a novice?

- If you're still too shy to read your own prose, select something you have confidence in. For that matter, read Shake-

speare aloud, as his language is so sensual you can't help but be inspired.
- Read aloud alone, not only with an audience.
- Read aloud, and then begin writing on the spot.
- Have your lovers read you the most arousing things in your library, and masturbate while they tell you the story.
- Memorize something erotic, and then recite it while slowly taking off your clothes, keeping your eyes entirely on your listener.
- Tell a story to someone every night.
- Whisper a very short story in your lover's ear.
- Travel to the ocean, or to a large cave or forest, and yell your most potent erotic verse.

Goal
- To discover the sexual and aural power of speaking erotic prose.
- To test literature you're unsure of. If it doesn't work out loud, it's not going to be successful for silent readers, either.
- To become as fluent speaking erotic language as you are writing it—one enhances the other.

After You Finish This Exercise, You'll Never Believe Again . . .
- That erotica is meant to be private.
- That speaking verse and prose is a dull exercise.
- That reading aloud is only for actors.
- That words can't be sex.

Some of you will want to dissent and excuse yourself from these efforts; you'll think I'm kidding or exaggerating. But I give you every one of these suggestions as my best advice for improving your writing and your love life. Reading aloud will change your writing life *and* your sex life. It doesn't matter whether you are good or bad at it, only that you do it.

Some of you will say that this approach is too touchy-feely—that you have an excellent command of the English language and you don't need any of these "amateur theatricals" to make your point.

Well, Mrs. Henning, if that's the case, you are going to stumble in your erotic ambitions. Erotica is the touchy-feely ne plus ultra, because sex is all about touching and feeling. It is a living, listening, and speaking tradition. All erotica is a stage, and we authors merely players on it. With this in mind, I advise you to learn your lines.

The Erotic Reader's Bill of Rights

My criterion for choosing the "best" erotica is simple enough—it must sweep me away. If it doesn't pass what author Dorothy Allison calls the "wet test" at first read, then it must haunt me later, at all kinds of strange hours.

What makes a great erotic story, one that makes the most weary libido twitch with anticipation? I propose an erotic reader's bill of rights, some straight talk about what's genuinely sexy and what's not.

• A Good Sex Story Is Something That Arouses the Author

That seems obvious enough in other genres—whoever heard of a chef writing a recipe for pickle relish when her true love was pastry?

All human beings have an inalienable right to compose their own sexual stories. Writing one's erotic memoir is one of the few activities in which nonwriters and professionals alike spontaneously put pen to paper and go for it.

Sometimes I receive copies of amateur erotic work in the mail, perhaps with the line "To Sylvia, forever" scrawled at the top. The authors want to share with me the piece they composed for their beloved. But even if I think the prose is corny or incomprehensible, a part of me always knows that this story meant more to Sylvia (and her lover) than any publishing contract could deliver.

People don't routinely write sonnets to their cars, or vulnerable confessions about their jobs, or fantasies about everlasting friendship. The novice pen comes out for birth, death, and lust; it's almost immaterial whether anyone else appreciates it. A piece of erotica might be turned down for lack of craft or substance, but it can't be rejected as an individual lover's moment of truth.

• A Great Erotic Story Never Succumbs to Clichés

So much nonsense is circulated about what is "sexy" that writers will often hide their own preferences behind superficial hype, or resort to genre chestnuts that are worn to the nub. Treacly romances for the "female audience" are one erotic disaster area, closely followed by literary lechery—the leering expectation that, by simply repeating a woman's measurements over and over again, some orgasmic effect will be achieved. The fact is, most tits-and-ass storytellers (aside from a few true lingerie fetishists) are a bunch of prudes. They love to scream "Fuck big tits" in a crowded theater, but you'll never find them actually doing it in a dark matinee.

Of course, there are successful erotic stories in every genre, but the character's erotic motives must have authentic and sensitive hooks that readers can relate to.

• A Great Erotic Story Is a Tease

I once got a good short lesson from a veteran stripper on how to undress for an audience: "Look 'em straight in the eyes, and slowly unbutton like you've got all day."

The finest erotic authors are the great tease artists. They get the readers hanging by their short hairs, then they spin them around and make them forget what they came for—only to pull them in again like so much taffy.

It helps to tell a story and to make a context that's bigger than "boy/girl meets girl/boy." In fact, that's the very thing you want to defeat—the reader's expectation that every erotic story is a predictable plot of people getting it on. The brilliant erotic story will make readers forget they ever had any expectations at all.

All readers approach an erotic story with a realistic prediction of what will occur. They know the protagonist has to get satisfied. But if your characters are compelling, and your plot is diabolically clever, then we won't be tempted to cruise for dirty words. A great erotic story will create a state of uncertainty in readers, no matter how smug they were when they opened the first page.

• A Great Erotic Story Has a Literary Climax

Everyone knows how brief the orgasmic moment is. But composing a good orgasm scene can take hours, weeks, forever. A fine erotic writer doesn't dare cop out of it. The days are gone when you could cut to "I woke up and had no idea where I was." You know damn well where you were, and if your character had a blackout, you'd better get someone else in the story to re-create the action.

Reading about an orgasm is always brief, perhaps even quicker than the real thing. Writers who insist on drawing it out for paragraphs, with detailed ocean metaphors and inner bursts of karmic sunlight, are killing it. The orgasm scene is the final shoe dropping from the prosy foreplay that you've been teasing us with all along. When that relief comes, it had better be exquisite, sweet—and brief.

• A Great Erotic Story Employs Clichés—at Just the Right Moment

It's easy to be cheesy about sex, and the population shares a collective cynicism about sexual stereotypes.

Ironically, the object of erotic foreplay is to get your reader in such a tizzy that, when the moment of truth arrives, your heroine can yell, "Take me now, Brad!" or "Hard-uh, deep-uh, fast-uh"—and the reader will love every second of it. There are certain expressions, like those above, or the classic "I love you," that can't be replaced by anything else, yet they can never be obvious or expected if they are to be successful.

Some writers, of course, subvert the pornographic and romantic punch lines by unabashedly using them in a satiric or pop culture onslaught, where we know it's obnoxious but we can't resist. In Mark Butler's "Cool and Clean and Crisp," from *Best American Erotica 1994*, our man doesn't mince pop in his climactic scene:

> We got into the Land Rover just as the storm hit, and she caught just enough rain to make her hair so sexy wet that we just had to do it one more time, so I strapped her down roughly in the back seat with safety belts as she pouted. Invitingly . . .
>
> I mounted her as she squirmed rain wet slippery silly under the bondage of state law, moaned, "Oh what a feeling!" and balanced our beer cans on her breasts. Then, as I drove her perfect willing ass into the soft Corinthian leather . . .

Satire aside, the best way to transform a killer cliché is with expert detail and imaginative description. In the *Best American Erotica 1994* story "Unsafe Sex," Pat Califia has her two male players talking the kind of trash you could hear in any two-dollar porn movie—but look how she leads into it:

> I make one more attempt to get what I really want, and he slaps my butt. Hard. So hard it takes my breath away. I hate that. Of course, it also makes my asshole open up like an umbrella. He's a marvelous fuck. It takes a lot of skill to drive something that big. Too many well-hung men think all they have to do is the old in and out. But this man is teasing me, stroking all points of the compass, doing everything inside of me except turning cartwheels. I wish it were enough, I really do. But I know he isn't going to lose his stinking, filthy load in me, really use me, soil and despoil me. And without the fillip of that violation and defilement, I can't let go.
>
> "You like come so much, I wanna see yours," he pants. "Get it out and jack it off, boy. Show your master how much you love taking his hard dick."

• A Great Erotic Story Includes Afterglow and Aftergrow

Many erotic writers have one place where they choke. Either they know how to talk dirty but can't leisurely play out the seduction—or else they have a beauty of a plot but start feeling embarrassed and stiff when the sex gets explicit. In either case, they might not have a plan for "life after climax"—and there certainly is one.

A lot of writers conclude a fabulous sex scene by metaphorically jumping out of the bed. They move their characters off somewhere where we can't see them, and do who knows what.

Once you've written your erotic climax, it's true you can't stay on that precipice. But coming down has its fine moments, and a good erotic writer won't ignore them. Erotic hindsight is always popular—how the characters look back on their bodies and their desire. If you have a strong story that's been supporting the sex the whole time, then you won't end with just a come stain on the sheets. I've rarely seen "and they lived happily ever after" work as a conclusion, but some authors have made a sick noirish twist on the old chestnuts. In her first book, *Dogs in Lingerie*, writer Danielle Willis concluded her satiric saga of teenage idol lust, "Elegy for Andy Gibb," by memorializing her biggest crush:

> Anyway, the day he died I was sitting in a torture chamber in Berkeley crossing and uncrossing my legs in agony because my golden shower client was almost 20 minutes late. I reached for the newspaper to distract me from my now almost uncontrollable urge to run to the bathroom and there on the front page of the entertainment section was the headline; ANDY GIBB DEAD OF NATURAL CAUSES AT AGE 30, along with an airbrushed photo of Andy in his heyday. He really was cute.

Part III

Writing It

How to Get Ideas

When erotic writers go blank, how are they different from any other authors who suffer from writer's block? There is no difference, unless the erotic authors are vulnerable to the notion that it's their subject matter that's holding them back, rather than their craft or imagination. Some writers think they haven't had enough sex, or enough "interesting sex," to compose a worthy erotic passage. Others, taking the "whore" counterpoint to the "virgin" point of view, believe they've had entirely too much sex; they fear they have written about it so relentlessly that there's simply nothing left to say. These authors, whether virgin or slut, each blame their subject, sex, for being either too elusive or too worn out to provide original material.

The Virgin

I once attended a social workers' seminar in a lumber mill region of northern California. A legal specialist asked the audience to break up into pairs for a little exercise. She told us to confide in our partner of the moment and tell him or her our most recent sexual experience. At the conclusion of the exercise, she told us she didn't think we'd actually do it, that she was only showing us how difficult it would be to testify about one's sexual experiences in court—but I had already taken her instructions in dead seriousness.

I was paired with a pale, large girl sitting next to me, who looked frightened out of her wits, so I offered to go first.

"I have a woman lover right now," I ventured, to see if that made her turn on her heel. She didn't flinch. "Lots of times I get ideas from books we read, and lately we've been reading all this stuff about whether S/M—sadomasochism," I said, spelling it out, searching her face to see how this was going over, "about whether it's all right or not."

She was so perfectly still, her blue eyes more opaque by the second, that I had to interrupt my story. "Do you want to hear this, or should I just shut up?"

"No, go ahead," she said, as if I was asking for a second helping.

I took my biggest breath yet. "So, I said to my girlfriend, 'Why don't we try this and find out whether it's totally evil or totally hot.'"

I told her my story of a somewhat silly but ultimately illuminating night of bondage experiments. It was my seatmate's turn now, and to my surprise, she started weeping. I was so ashamed of myself—what was I thinking? How could I come up to this seminar on child abuse and talk about my San Francisco lesbo adventures? I was nuts.

"I've never had sex," she whispered, wiping her eyes.

All my conceit and kinky self-consciousness crumbled at her four-word confession. She was visibly shrinking.

"But you just mean you haven't had sex with another person!" I said, fumbling for Kleenex in my pocket. "I'm sure you've had lots of sexual experiences with yourself, in your fantasies and your own body. Everybody has a story."

She didn't lift her chin from her chest, but she nodded. "I do," she said.

I dipped the top of my head against hers.

I can still plainly remember the sexual fantasies that I spun in my head before a single soul had ever kissed or touched me. They were among the most powerful erotic experiences of my life. There is no such thing as a person who doesn't have an erotic autobiography. I feel as if I'm opening up Pandora's little jewel box every time I open my mind to write an erotic scene.

I wish I could have shown that mill-town girl an essay that Greta Christina wrote called "Are We Having Sex Now or What?" in an anthology called *The Erotic Impulse*. In it she explores, in detail, how what the status quo calls "having sex" differs from actual profound sexual experience:

> The problem was, as I kept doing more kinds of sexual things, the line between *sex* and *not-sex* kept getting more hazy and indistinct. As I brought more into my sexual experience, things were showing up on the dividing line demanding my attention. It wasn't just that the territory I labeled "sex" was expanding. The line itself has swollen, dilated, been transformed into a vast gray region. It had become less like a border and more like a demilitarized zone . . .
>
> I know when I'm *feeling* sexual. I'm feeling sexual if my pussy's wet, my nipples are hard, my palms are clammy, my brain is fogged, my skin is tingly and super-sensitive, my butt muscles clench, my heartbeat speeds up. I have an orgasm (that's the real give-away), and so on. But feeling sexual with someone isn't the same as having sex with them. Good Lord, if I called it sex every time I was attracted to someone who returned the favor, I'd be even more bewildered than I am now. Even *being* sexual with someone isn't the same thing as *having* sex with them. I've danced and flirted with too many people, given and received too many sexy, would-be-seductive back rubs, to believe otherwise.

Children can write about their sexual feelings, and so can the aged, the ill, the cloistered and closeted, and everyone else whom we don't commonly give sexual credibility to. People who've only had bad sex still experience pleasure and complexity, in their memories and in their bodies. Writers who've only had sex one time in their lives, or with only one person in all their lives, still have a fantasia of dreams and sensations that could touch a million lovers.

I decided to begin *The Best American Erotica 2000* with a story by a woman who announces at the onset, "I am 28 years old and I am a virgin." Author Debra Boxer then goes on to describe the ways she imagines having sex, which are full of her womanly body and adult desire:

> People assume a series of decisions led to this. They guess that I'm a closet lesbian, or too picky, or clinging to a religious ideal. "You don't look, talk, or act like a virgin," they say. For lack of a better explanation, I am pigeonholed as a prude or an unfortunate. If it's so hard to believe, I want to say, then imagine how hard it is for me to live with . . .
>
> There are sudden passions that form in my mind when I look at a man. Thoughts of things I want to do to him. I want to follow the veins of his wrists—blue like the heart of a candle flame. I want to lick the depression of his neck as if it were the bottom of a bowl. I want to see the death of my modesty in his eyes. Although I am swollen with romantic ideas, I am not naïve. I know it will not be ideal. Rather it will be bloody, painful, awkward, damp, and dreadful—but this is always the way of birth. It is an act of violence. The threat of pain in pleasure, after all, makes seduction stimulating. I want the pain, to know that I am alive and real—to leave no doubt there has been a transformation.

The Worn-out Slut—Writers Who've Eroticized Too Much

Many experienced sex writers might read about the aforementioned virgin and weep with envy. Wouldn't it be great to feel so brand spanking new—to be bounding about like a Madonna, "touched for the very first time"? But instead you may feel crusty, mined out, as if you've crawled through every fold in the sexual psyche. Now you would just like a smooth place to lie down without anyone rubbing up against you.

The desire for rest is genuine. When you feel like this about sex writing, you are burned-out, and I would bet that it's not the only creative juice that's run low. It would be a mistake to blame your ennui on sex, per se, as if it were a catalog you had simply indexed to the last tedious page. Erotic writing is not like going to the doctor's office—it isn't a literature of pathology; it's not a set of bugs that require a limited number of labels and jars.

There are two kinds of erotic burnout for experienced sex writers. One—and this is unfortunately the most common—happens when you're writing formula stories for a publisher that has a little bible of things you can't write about and a repetitive jingle of what you can.

At first, it can be a bit of a challenge to learn the code, then push it to its outer limits. Finally you realize that, no matter what you do, you're still "knit one, purl two."

You say to yourself, "Okay, this isn't creative, it's a job, just keep the fingers moving on the keyboard." You may find yourself enjoying a bit of perverse smugness that you can write so consistently in a format you frankly despise.

Yet you're kidding yourself if you believe that becoming a master hack will not affect your creative process. You aren't running the game; it's running you—at a terrific loss. You may be "writing," but you're not creating; you've abandoned authenticity, and what's worse, it's abandoned you.

The less common erotic block for writers is that of authors who have health issues or time conflicts that have saddled them with preemptive fatigue.

I'm the first one to tell people to write "every day," but, in fact, you need to *not* write some days; you need weekends and holidays and sabbaticals. There's no special cure for the tired writer other than to simply live a little without writing about it. Do anything you want, be as productive or slothful as you please, but don't *write* at all. Before you know it, you'll have another great idea you want to pen down.

Let's go back to the uglier problem—the author who's written seventy titles and seven hundred short scenes that are all the same recipe, but with different hair colors and toenail polish. You've finally said, *Enough!* You want to enjoy a meaningful writing recovery.

By all means, if you want to childishly blame it on "sex," go ahead and have a sex-writing moratorium for a while—as long as you keep writing about something. You'll find that the "something" will inevitably turn sexual if you aren't deliberately cutting off its natural course. Human drama and comedy turn to the sexual without any artificial maneuvers.

While you can (and certainly will) burn out on rigid formulas (TV sitcom scripts, for example), you will never exhaust a meaty subject (for example, a family of six tries to make a go of it). In other words, if one could say and do anything they wanted with the Brady Bunch, it would be endlessly inspirational and entertaining. But the formula in which TV shows are written doesn't allow that spectrum; in fact, it's more dictatorial than any sex book formula I've ever heard of.

Sex isn't a writing problem, but hack writing and fatigue are. Address your real writing enemies, and enjoy the creative bounty of your subject material.

Writing Exercises to Get New Ideas

Writing exercises are like parlor games—they're fun, they're a bit contrived, and yet the goal is to trip yourself into spontaneity. They're the icebreakers in the conversation between your unconscious and your keyboard.

I love writing games—I could make up a new one every day, because I dearly love improvisations. Just like improv, the one thing that can stop people from enjoying it is to question the process up front, to become a critic rather than a participant.

Yet once you begin as a writer, rather than an ironic observer, you can deviate in any direction you want. Once you're writing, and your head is buzzing with what you want to say next, there's no need to drag yourself back to the parameters of the original exercise.

Let me introduce you to one of my favorite writing exercises. Again, use it as a jumping-off point—it's immaterial whether you follow it to the letter or go off on a different path, as long as you start writing!

FANTASIES EXERCISE

Give yourself two minutes to answer each of the following questions. When your time is up, stop, even if you haven't finished your sentence.

- Write down an erotic fantasy about a sexual experience that you would have in a minute if it were offered to you, no questions asked. It should be something you would have no reservations or conditions about doing in real life.
- Write down an erotic fantasy about a sexual experience that you would only have under certain conditions. You could give yourself up wholeheartedly under these conditions, but otherwise not at all.
- Write down an erotic fantasy about a sexual experience that is completely satisfying to you in your imagination but that you could not do because it is either physically impossible or something you could never bring yourself to do in real life . . . Yet in your mind, it is completely hot and fulfilling.

Now you have three potential pieces of fiction, based on your fantasies. Take another sheet of paper and answer the following:

- What do you notice about the differences, or similarities, between your three fantasies?
- Have you ever confided any of these fantasies to anyone?
- Is any one of your three fantasies more compelling than another, sexually or creatively?

Goal
- To articulate thoughts that are often unspoken and unwritten.
- To pay intimate attention to your erotic unconscious.
- To identify the elements in your erotic "stories" that both propel you and inhibit you.

After You Finish This Exercise, You'll Never Believe Again . . .
- That your fantasy life is barren.
- That fantasies can only be satisfied by acting them out.
- That fantasies are not enhanced by conflicts, taboos, and inhibitions. (Like literature, they thrive on all those things!)

THE "FAVORITE WRITER" EXERCISE

The best exercise for creative inspiration is to enjoy other artists' work and interpretations. Many writers feel guilty for all the books they read instead of writing, the movies they watch instead of writing, the music they listen to instead of writing. But these are the very activities that galvanize us. Our "originality" is nothing more than our unique response to everyone we ever wanted to imitate or seduce.

I don't mind erring on the side of self-indulgence in this matter. I love to hear about famous authors who are gluttons for more words, more pictures, more singing and dancing. You need to make time for all of it.

- Schedule yourself to write. Write every day you can.
- Don't write *every* day—schedule regular days off. Live without writing on occasion.
- Beware of formats and formulas—you may master them, but they will cauterize you.
- Don't think you've exhausted a worthy subject—and sex is the ultimate worthy subject.
- Read, listen, and observe to your heart's content.
- Experience sexuality, behold it in your own eyes and with every other sense in your body.
- Don't wonder how much sex is enough, or too much. Let the truth of the situation determine the power of imagination.

Goal

- To lay the foundation for a writer's discipline.
- To appreciate reading, and listening, for what it can give to your writing.
- To appreciate sex for what it can give to your writing.
- To humble your inhibitions and fears in the face of your determination to write.

After You Finish This Exercise, You'll Never Believe Again . . .

- That writing is just for days you feel something special.
- That writing virtually every day is impossible—once you start the habit, it will feel impossible NOT to write every day.
- That there's nothing new to say about sex.
- That sex isn't good for thinking and writing—and vice versa!

How to Use the Whole (Fucking) English Language

It's a very old complaint that English doesn't have the variety and nuance of vocabulary to refine the sexual experience creatively. Many writers feel that they are given two choices in their language: vulgar versus prissy, with neither conveying the complexity they had in mind. Yet after struggling with this difficulty myself, I've come to believe that this complaint is based more on laziness and prudishness than anything else.

English, like every language, has wonderful innuendoes and descriptions for the most intimate parts of our lives and bodies. Our Anglo-Saxon words for body parts and functions are some of the strongest, most influential, and common words in our language.

For example, the word *fuck*, originally from the Old English term *foken*, meaning to beat or hit against, is used all over the world by other language speakers who, once hearing it in vernacular, realize that there is nothing that compares with its universally understood aggressiveness, its potential to both insult and excite.

When it comes to the forbidden nature of sex words, the female terms are even more taboo than the male ones. Many people who would say, "Penis, dick, cock" without blinking turn to mush when confronted with "Clitoris, pussy, cunt." Everything about women's sexuality, from reproduction to pleasure, is more mysterious, carries more superstition, and is more taboo. This makes the language of women's sexuality, whether medical jargon or street slang, something that gets avoided.

I once had a terrific fight on an AOL author chat because the producers told me that "penis" was an acceptable term to use to the audience, but "clitoris" was not. On the other side, Eve Ensler's *Vagina Monologues* has probably been the most-talked-about stage show of the decade, because both its title and its subject demand a positive, unapologetic attention to the language of women's sex. An entire book by Inga Muscio, titled *Cunt*, has found itself in the peculiar position of receiving rave reviews from critics and feminists, who then can't print the title of the book in the publication in which they're offering their review!

Writers have struggled over sexual language and stereotypes because we've agonized so fiercely over how to keep our readers' attention while not offending them entirely. We want our words to break the radio and TV barrier, to be heard instead of bleeped. Yet the only way to make progress in appreciating these words in context is to use them. Plays like *Vagina Monologues*, or books like *Cunt*, have been breakthrough successes because their authors believed it was time to throw down the linguistic gauntlet. The fact is, words about women's sexual bodies have been far more suppressed than the analogous terms for men. But regardless of gender, writers, by necessity of the truth, need to use the entire English language—at its most coarse, visceral, and blatant—in complete integration with its most tender and delicate forms.

Look how Marianna Beck, in her story "C Is for Closet, Crevice and Colossus," in *The Best American Erotica 1994*, manages to refer to a woman's pussy eight times in succession without ever making us weary, always learning a bit more (italics are mine):

She stepped right over me, naked except for her brassiere, and provided me with a direct shot of her *furry cleft*. Up until then I'd only heard about *these things*. My mother had once referred to a woman's *Schmuckkästchen—the little jewel box*—in relation to some neighbor who was pregnant. So I naturally thought that females possessed *something with a lid which they regularly flipped open to have children*. What I saw was decidedly much different, something considerably more *alive, forbidden, mysterious—something I wanted to touch*. I wanted to know what those *puffy banks of hair* felt like and where that *thin dark crevice* disappeared to between her legs.

Pornographic language is often a spike to a more indirect volley. Look at Anne Tourney finishing off her sex scene in "Full Metal Corset," from the same volume:

"This time I'll reward you," he says. He seizes her knees, spreads them and leans down to cleave her lips with his tongue. Removing his tongue from her steaming hole, he spears her clit with it. She comes in seconds.

"Cleave her lips" is arty. "Steaming hole" is nasty. Yet the author moves easily from one point to the next, without preciousness or discrimination. She has created a riveting description that is neither monotonous nor patronizing. She has brought the dynamics of language to her characters' bodies.

Many professional writers, being pragmatists, insist that if their words are going to be censored anyway, they might as well be the ones to compose reasonable, more vanilla alternatives. But this is a strategy of self-censorship, and it will defeat your storytelling in more ways than surrendering a word or two will.

Yes, you can choose to make changes in the edit, as your publisher may demand once the story is composed. But the first time, write the story the way it demands to be told! Use the words that your authentic characters would use. Don't play the preacher and rewrite your story for an imaginary offended audience, let alone an offended God. This is your best chance to present your story in all its glory.

The biggest trend among aficionados of classic literature is to dig up the original works and to publish the unexpurgated version, un-mangled by religious language censors. The original *Aesop's Fables* can now be found, with none of the "morals" and all of the sexual interest that appeared in the Greek originals:

> The Hyenas
> They say hyenas change their nature annually, and are sometimes male and sometimes female. In fact, a male hyena once showed unnatural inclinations toward a female hyena, and she said to him, "Very well, my friend, but remember that whatever you do now you will soon have done to you."—*Aesop Without Morals*

This movement to be honest about the "classics" is happening because popular culture has been so demanding of truth in language. Whether it's David Mamet thrashing sexual politics in his play *Oleanna*, or the latest hip-hop raconteur, no contemporary artist is interested in "mincing" his or her words for an anachronistic imaginary Vatican.

What's interesting these days is that, even though sexual slang is frequently used to hurl invective and disdain, it's still rare to find it used in its original lusty meanings. The MPAA rates movies PG if they use a word like *fuck* to curse someone; but if that same word is used to express sexual desire, the movie gets an R.

Lazy Curses

There's only one wrong way to use profane or carnal language, and that's out of laziness or as a gratuity. Like comedians who get dissed because they resort to a "dirty word" to get a laugh, writers of all kinds also get heat when they appear to be using *shit* or *goddamn* just as a way to worm out of stating something more articulately. We are often tempted to use dirty words for emphasis, like *very* or *really*, as red flags to tell the reader that we want their urgent attention. But you can never get readers to pay attention by begging them or shocking them, at least not for more than one round.

DIRTY WORDS EXERCISE

As a writer, you need to feel that your words are your tools, and you never want to be in a place where you're afraid to touch them. Even if you're the sort of person who doesn't see why you would ever need to use the word "cocksucker" in a sentence, being *uncomfortable* about using it is a different thing from *choosing* not to use it. Your language is your domain. You don't want to be nervous to travel anywhere in your vocabulary.

- If there are any words that scare you—words you've never said aloud or written down—write them down, in a list. Now write them over, a dozen-plus times, in your journal, at your keyboard, on the blackboard. Write them in caps, with fat felt pens—the more overt, the better.
- Observe your reactions before you begin your list, then during your "mouthing off," and finally, after you've completed it. Now write about THAT.
- Compose a 250–550 word scene in which the most taboo words in your vocabulary are used with reckless disregard. Your story must have both a male and a female character who use these words in dialogue.
- Read the above story scene out loud to yourself.
- Read it out loud to someone else.
- Now have a good laugh about it all.

Goal

- To break the intimidating hold any taboo word has over you.
- To get the preachers and finger-waggers out of your head permanently.

After You Finish This Exercise, You'll Never Believe Again . . .

- That there's any such thing as a "bad" word.
- That once you use vulgar language, you'll lose your light touch.
- That any words you use in your writing define you, rather than your story.

Making Up a New Vocabulary

Some people think they're going to create new words as a way of escaping the tyranny of the old ones, but I strongly caution you to avoid this conceit. Yes, some writers are famous for creating "new" words, like sci-fi master Robert Heinlein did with *grok*, his verb for making a deeply sympathetic personal connection. But he was successful with his word invention because he created such a believable world in *Stranger in a Strange Land*. In the 1960s search for communality and inner meaning, his word was so appropriate that it made its way into the mainstream lexicon.

Most writers are not going to hit such perfect timing with their characterizations. Even *grok* went out of fashion eventually, and outside its generation of sci-fi fans and hippies, most people don't know it today.

Most "new" words gain in popularity because they are clever modifications of old ones, or they are based on something or someone in the news, making an impact. The *gate* part of "Watergate Hotel" became a synonym for political scandal; the name Trump created a one-syllable connotation for greed and unfettered capitalism. "I'll show you my Bill if you'll show me your Monica" makes instant sense to anyone alive during the Starr Report, and it's perfectly in keeping with our puritanical tradition of using code words to refer to our genitals.

Sex and politics are probably the areas of language most influenced by gossip—they are the fastest changing and most adaptive parts of English. Maybe that's why I love both those topics so much, because they're so fertile in the vocabulary department. I like the way our historical repression of English sexual vocabulary has created its own backlash. Our cultural sense of naughtiness, of euphemism, and of winking metaphor has created a tremendous wealth of sexual connotation that would otherwise be banished entirely.

Don't fret over language—flog it and flaunt it! The practice of storytellers is what keeps English alive, and it's the very reason why anyone bothers to listen.

Sexual Character

A memorable erotic story has a memorable lover inside it—in fact, if your story or scene is remembered for anything, it will be for one of its characters.

When we try to remember a great book we once read, even if we don't remember the title or the author, we will try to recall it by saying, "It's about those two drifters who killed a whole family in the middle of nowhere," or "It's about that woman who ruined everyone around her in order to save her plantation." We don't remember novels by the weather, or their sheer lyricism, and we don't even explain their plots without emphasizing a main character's destiny.

Luckily for writers, creating characters does come somewhat naturally, because it's a natural part of telling any kind of story. Creating outstanding characters—personalities who are legendary—is the focus of this chapter.

I think of my characters' voices as the most priceless extension of my once-favorite childhood pastime: playing with my dolls. My Barbie, Midge, and Skipper were a blistering triangle, and you could count on my Clownie and Bear to weigh in whenever there was a doll crisis.

Where did my mannequins' personalities come from? I'm sure some of their qualities imitated those of the adults around me. Then, as I began reading and became infatuated with storybook characters, I would incorporate my favorite bit of *B'rer Rabbit* or *Harriet the Spy*. Blond Betty and raven-haired Veronica from the *Archie* comics were probably my first templates for Midge and Barbie. Even then, I had the basic good-girl/bad-girl cliché set up, where one female was more manipulative and reckless than the other—yet she managed consistently to get the man, instead of the responsible, nice girl.

My own weakness with character development, which is a common one: my impatience, my desire to take a shortcut that "no one will notice"—but they always do. The reason English teachers are always harping on the maxim, Show, Don't Tell is that *telling* your audience what your characters are like is much faster than showing them anything, but never improves the story!

It only takes me a few seconds to say, "Barbie is a sleazy gold digger." Great, now I've told you; I've taken away a bit of a puzzle and discovery I might have given to my reader.

But if I decide to demonstrate Barbie's dubious ethics, I'll have a much bigger challenge—but a lot more excitement for my reader. If I persevere, my patience in showing her actions will captivate my audience. Otherwise, they may drop my story after a couple of pages of my "telling" them what my characters are like.

When I am reading one of my own first drafts, one of the first things I look for is declarative sentences and descriptions that are backed up by nothing. I always find plenty of them, and I lambaste myself for it—that's what my second pass is for; I look for all the places where I sped by, dropping a clue without finishing the puzzle.

I've also noticed how popular it is, in contemporary writing, to drop in a brand name or a celebrity name to give instant character background. If you say in your story, "Britney Spears pulled up on her Vespa, wearing her Calvin Klein thong," your pop-culture-addict audience will get a momentary kick out of the fact that they know all the gossip about three different elements in your story. However, it's arrogant to assume that your readers read the *National Enquirer*. Your blasé celebrity witticisms are going to wear pretty thin if you don't create unique interpretations and motives for the actors on your page.

Real people (our family and friends) and mythical people (our

- That fictional characters aren't based on composites of people the author has known very well.
- That Monica Lewinsky and my aunt Molly couldn't possibly have cruised each other at the post office.

Erotic Characters

Erotic characters are virtually impossible to create without referring to our sexual mythology. As authors, we're either speaking to stereotypes like the virgin versus the whore, or we're rebelling against them. Even the male characters have a double standard: We have the brutal cad, the callow youth, the mean yucky guy dames fall for like rain—or the sweet boy, the devoted hubby, the Clark Kent, who strives to get the girl, sometimes catches her, but doesn't seem to get all that lusty about it.

Nice guys not only have a harder time getting sex, they also seem to have a harder time touching ecstasy. In our society's legends, bad people get punished, but they also seem to get laid; the nice heroes win the day, but they also seem too squeaky clean to have fun—what happened to their libidos?

Many contemporary writers, and feminist writers in particular, have been so outraged by the sex-negative connotations of these legends that they have resolved to do away with them altogether. They are determined to write about a saint who gets horny and a villain who never gets hard.

Both these sound like ideas for great stories—but not because they are prescriptions for sexism. Rather, a promiscuous saint and a villain without balls are interesting because they're both protagonists who face a challenge in what people expect from them. How they solve that conundrum is your plot, and their destiny is your conclusion. Take care that your characters should have a full life; don't let them become "spokespeople" for a message, instead of real people dealing with intimate challenges.

Beware the Agenda

The number one sin of postfeminist erotic writing has been to create characters that serve a political agenda rather than a believable plot line. An editor called me not long ago to say that she had a great idea for an anthology: a whole series of stories about happy monogamous couples who still find each other attractive and have never felt pulled in any direction besides each other's bedside. I choked, then I struggled to tell her that such an idea was courting literary disaster— a two-pound paperweight of tedium.

Is this because I'm against happiness, monogamy, and marriage? No, my writerly fears have nothing to do with my "positions" on these subjects as parts of the human condition. The problem is that, if your story opens with a complete state of satisfaction, and closes with the same—without a ripple in between—where's the story? An uninterrupted smile is as tiresome as a permanent frown. You don't have to make the happy couple divorce or murder each other in order to create reader interest. But one of your lovers needs to have a doubt, a problem, or a conflict in order for the story to breathe.

Empathize, Don't Demonize

Just because you have a struggle in your plot doesn't mean you get to hand out the black and white hats and let the story hasten to its final judgment.

One book I reviewed recently, *The Sharp Edge of Love: Erotic Passions of Submissive Women*, tells the story of a suburban guy who realizes his true sexual nature as an erotic Dominant, and who goes about meeting and seducing a series of captivating, yet challenging, submissive women. So far, so good. The Dom and his girlfriends are triangulated by the actions of the Dom's ex-wife, who discovers his kinky closet life; she sets out to destroy his business, to cut off his contact with his kids, and to make him a pariah in their old community. Clearly, there's enough drama and pathos in this autobiography to keep anyone awake all night . . . except for one thing.

The author has made the wife into a perfect cardboard villain and the husband into a surprised innocent victim. So we get the message loud and clear—"Hell hath no fury like a scorned ex-wife" or "Coming out of the closet is the bravest thing you'll ever do"—but the story is compromised by lazy character development.

The author wrote a reply to me and said he was stung by my criticism. He ventured that I had never been sexually persecuted in this way by a family member, and that if I had, I would never doubt him.

I replied, "But it's not your real life I doubt, it's your storytelling that's at issue." It doesn't matter whether I was born yesterday or whether I've walked a hundred miles in your shoes—you have to create believable, authentic characters, not good-versus-evil cartoons, if you're going to get your message across. Don't tell me the wife is a bitch; show me her true colors by telling me her story! Tell me why you married her in the first place. This is the complexity it takes to hook the reader—both to your story and to your "side."

In both storytelling and real life, deep wounds begin before conflict reaches its climax. It would be much juicier to find out, for example, that the ex-wife has kinky fantasies she's never told anyone, or that her husband once sexually rejected her when she was vulnerable. Somewhere in her character, sex matters to her, even though she is the frigid villain, and we have to know that about her in order to make her persona come alive. Similarly, knowing how the husband once loved someone like her—and desired her, or betrayed her—will make him a deeper and ultimately more sympathetic figure.

Instead, we have a hero saying that his woman done him wrong—

all because she is unenlightened about S/M—whereas he has seen the light. That doesn't make us like him, it just makes us wonder what her side of the story is.

You can't help gravitating toward one of your characters who is the "conscience" of the book, the one who most sympathetically expresses your ideals or philosophy. This is attractive not only to Pollyannas and devotees of the politically correct—it's also the temptation of writers who love their villains, or who relish satire and downbeat endings.

But you must always poke a hole or two in your hero, as well as make us feel the weight that Darth Vader may be carrying. Your nice girls must have their moment of spite; your femme fatales have to curl up and suck their thumbs every once in a while. I'd love to read the explicit erotic story of Joan of Arc—you can't go wrong with sex and martyrdom—and I'm eager to hear how Casanova faces his denouement.

"Show" me everything, and don't "tell" me a thing. If nothing else, prove to me that your characters, for all their valor or villainy, are truly just a bundle of contradictions.

Steamy Plots

The most contentious accusation that erotic writers face is the argument that sexually arousing stories do not require a plot at all. "Who needs to study story line?" the doubters proclaim. "You're only writing a dirty story!"

The skeptics say that if you just pile up the body parts and four-letter words onto the page, readers will soon be mopping their brows, and then they'll toss the story aside as soon as they've ejaculated, like a used condom. Once these readers come to their senses, they presumably move on to some "real" literature, to refresh themselves after their fling in the pig trough.

One book critic, in an *Esquire* review of *Best American Erotica 1994*, wrote, "If it's good art, it isn't good porn." This parochial school of critical thought holds that good smut—because of its orgasmic result—cannot excel at prose. There's the whole mind/body split laid out for you, a perfect aerial view.

First of all, it's true that erotica does not require a plot, any more than any writing subject requires a plot. If you do not want to use a narrative style in your sexual storytelling, perhaps it's because you choose to write in an experimental form. Maybe you are a poet. It would be your conscious decision not to use traditional plot devices, essentially like a musician choosing jazz over pop. It requires tremendous technique to be good at experimental forms, and if that's where your true interest lies, you needn't endure an internship of strictly narrative writing.

However, if writers approach erotica and decide to ditch their craft because they think erotica is "easier," or think they will be able to cut corners—then they need to stop kidding themselves. Sex won't function as a fuzzy aphrodisiac to cloud the reader's mind.

There is something about the ecstasy and emotional tenderness of sexual writing that intimidates authors; perhaps it has this in common with writing about death, birth, or "seeing God." Yet people who are writing about a near-death experience would never excuse sloppy writing by saying, "I didn't think plot was important because the experience was so intense that it speaks for itself."

No story "speaks for itself"—the author creates its voice, its timing, its surprises, and its climax. The more "intense" your subject is, the more care you must take to articulate its discovery.

Let's say you have a great sexual idea that you know is dramatic, and it's erotically audacious enough to rivet any audience. Suppose you've become aware of the trend for women to wax their body hair, in particular their pubic hair. You've seen that this is sexually exciting for some of the women on the receiving end—pain mixed with pleasure. Just saying the words out loud, "Hot burning wax," is enough to make most people squirm, so you know you've got a compelling topic.

Let me quote a couple of sentences from Ginu Kamani's short story "Waxing the Thing," from her book *Junglee Girl*, where she describes the thoughts of a girl working in a beauty parlor:

Of course it's my job to get all the hair out, but I can't help it, sometimes the hair just won't come out. I try once or twice, but these fussy ladies are never satisfied. For half an hour I have to feel around bit by bit for any leftover hair, and then when I find it, how can I wax just one hair? So I have to try to pull it out with my fingers, but even that is impossible because by then the skin has become all sensitive and slippery and sliding.

Then Mrs. Yusuf, my god, the way she shouts! "I can feel it, I can feel one hair, not there, other side, in the front, no, no, feel properly, grab the skin with one hand and pull with the other, try again, just wipe your fingers if they're sliding, don't think you can rush away without finishing your job," and on and on. What to do? I don't like digging around in there because I know it's where babies and all come from. But I don't grumble because the fussy ladies always give a good tip. Thank god they are not all like that or I would have to spend the whole day waxing and cleaning the thing of just one of them!

Kamani's story is not so successful because she picked a kinky topic. Her story is wonderful from beginning to end because she creates a whole world for us to look into before we even get to the melting point. Her story describes the awakening of a poor, uneducated village girl in India, who comes to the city and gets a chance to make some money for herself by servicing the richest women in town, who visit the beauty parlor for their hair-removal treatments.

Our heroine is completely unconscious of her own sexuality, yet she can't help being struck by the way some clients are fanatical about having her touch them in this extremely intimate way. She chalks up their patronage to her work ethic and her growing sense of what is "proper" for a woman, but in her naïve recounting of all she has seen, the reader clearly understands that our heroine is having a sexual experience, as much as she is having an education in gender and class relations.

Sure, the waxing bits are funny, arousing, and squirm-worthy. But they grace a story that has a character so believable you feel like she's sitting right next to you—a story that offers a whole commentary on women's relationship to beauty, pain, and sex. The fact that Kamani has so many things going on—a cultural biography, a social commentary, a funny story, a sex story—only makes each part flatter the others. The sex makes the politics more aching; the politics makes the sex more palatable.

Think of your plot as an erotic device. Every story line has a buildup, a conflict, a climax, and a conclusion, just like the physiological arc of an orgasm. If you don't have an "orgasmlike" literary structure to your story, then you don't have a story at all.

Put Sex in the (Story) Driver's Seat

Every act of making love is like a little play. Your plot, in all its design, is like a mirror of a sexual epiphany. For your story to reach a satisfying end, you need every stage. Don't write a sex scene as if you were pinning a gratuitous accessory to your fabric. Rather, insist that your sex scene drive the story forward somehow. If you could take the sex scene out of your overall story, and never even notice it was gone, then you didn't have any business writing that scene to begin with.

You can use sex at every point in the story. You can use sex to set the scene, to establish the characters, to create the conflict, to lay out the climax, to settle the conclusion. The filmmaker David Cronenberg told me in an interview that, when he made the film *Crash*, he was interested in seeing how he could drive a story forward entirely with sex scenes, from one act to the next. In a sense, he wanted to use pornographic film structure to tell an entire cinematic story.

This technique may be avant-garde in film, but erotic literature has been doing the same thing for a long time. The notorious example is *The Story of* O. The novel is nothing but sex scenes, yet each scene develops the plot exactly as I've described above. If you cut one sex act out of O's story, you would miss an important plot point. (The movie version didn't do this nearly as well.) The climax isn't when O is having sex again somewhere—but rather when she has to face the dilemma of pleasing her beloved master, yet allowing him to give her entirely away. This decision is her surrender, not her flushed

cheeks on any given page. It's the cruelty and sacrifice of her surrender that makes the novel so memorable.

STEAMY PLOT EXERCISE

Writing plots is an inevitable result of becoming conscious of them. If you feel uncertain of how plots work, take
a few examples of novels or movies that you enjoy, and dis-
sect them.

- Pick any famous novel or movie script that you know well.
- Pinpoint the scenes where you believe (examples in
  parentheses):
  The scene is set. (A man and woman find themselves
      alone in an idyllic garden.)
  The characters are established. (An ask-no-questions kind
      of guy is annoyed by his partner's constant curiosity;
      both are intimidated by a powerful, capricious garden
      keeper and a provocative viper.)
  The conflict is struck. (The woman wants fruit from the
      one tree in the garden they're not supposed to touch.)
  The climax is reached. (The snake convinces the woman
      to grab a bite of forbidden fruit.)
  The conclusion is reached. (The garden keeper throws the
      couple out and sentences them to a generational eter-
      nity of living with the results of their disobedience.)

- Take a story sample of your own writing, and subject it to
  the same analysis.
- Show your story to a friend or mentor, and ask the same
  questions. Do they find the same plot points as you?

Goal

- To look at your plot like a forensic scientist looks at a body—what happened here?
- To demystify the common elements to all plots, regardless of length or notoriety.
- To share constructive criticism with fellow readers and writers.

After You Finish This Exercise, You'll Never Believe Again . . .

- That high and low literature have entirely different designs.
- That it's impossible, or ill-advised, to deconstruct your own writing.
- That any two people tell, or read, a familiar story exactly the same way.

Flailing

What if you read your own story and see that a key element is missing—the conflict, the climax, a satisfactory conclusion? You've worked on this story for weeks, and you can't see straight anymore, let alone find a cure for your plot failure.

I often find that when I'm at the end of my rope with a story, only direct action will get me out of my rut. Plot ruts are essentially those times when you lose confidence and momentum. What you need isn't so much the perfect answer to your riddle as much as a shove.

THE CLICHÉ-RIDDEN PLOT-BUSTER EXERCISE

- Find the category below that addresses the hole in your story. Under each category is a series of operatic plot choices. Pick one—with a roll of the dice, if necessary.

Conflict

Your protagonist gets sick.

Your protagonist isn't happy at home anymore.

Your protagonist finds out s/he isn't who s/he thought s/he was.

Climax

Your protagonist learns s/he will die in six months.

The house burns down with everyone but the protagonist in it.

The protagonist learns that her/his real family is from disgraced royal blood.

Conclusion

The protagonist travels to the afterlife and returns to tell the tale.

The protagonist finds one survivor of the deadly fire.

The protagonist is crowned as the new king/queen.

- Take the cliché you've chosen and insert it into the hole in your story, right where the action begins to lag.
- Insist on cramming this stupid cliché into your story line. It won't fit—of course, it's not your idea! Write a couple of paragraphs around the concept, using everything you know about your primary characters. Have some fun with it.

- Congratulate yourself. At this point, you have a conflict (or a climax, or a resolution) where none existed before. It's not the right one, but you have foiled your writer's block.
- Now, throw that stupid cliché out and write a new conflict/climax/ending. It doesn't have to be the "right" one, but it will undoubtedly be better than the one I provided you!
- Write another one. By this time, you'll know what feels right, because you will have rejected the absurd, as well as a first draft.
- Continue with your rewrite. Go beyond the hole. Sleep on it, and in a few days, fine-tune it again.

Goal
- To break the terror regime of a plot stumbling-block.
- To find multiple choices for your characters, instead of the overrated "only right choice."
- To continue writing when you don't know where you're heading.

After Your Finish This Exercise, You'll Never Believe Again . . .
- That you're helpless in the face of plot failure.
- That only one idea can save your story, if only you could think of it.
- That being ridiculous has no place in serious (not to mention erotic) literature.

Seeing Ahead

Plots are easy to see in retrospect, but they're not always such a snap to plan in advance. As a writer, you can become so enamored of one stage in your story—say, establishing the characters—that you lose proportion and steam when it comes to taking those great characters and going somewhere. Or you may know all about your climax but have little idea how it came to pass.

When I have one part of a story worked out well in my mind, I don't torture myself by staving it off—I write the chapter that I want to write. It invariably helps me to understand what comes before and after. At other times you may find yourself in a perfect chronological lockstep, or following your outline like a conductor with a baton. There's no one right way. You can write like an indulged child as long as you (or someone else) edit your work like a fascist martinet. Writing your inspiration will preserve your spontaneity; editing will provide the chance to be ruthless, to bring all your elements into blissful order.

Climax

Every story, erotic or not, has a literary climax.

In erotic storytelling, that climax may be literally orgasmic, combining the peak of its narrative with a sexual peak for its characters. But whether your orgasm scene arrives on the first page, or at the climax, or in the last paragraph, you need to make the sexual climax as emotionally believable as anything in real life. You want to enhance, rather than defy, the high point of your story.

In real life, people experience sexual peaks in every emotional shading. Orgasm is not always breathless, happy, or romantic—it could just as well be stoic, melancholy, or alienated. The most misunderstood notion of the literary or cinematic orgasm is the cliché that it must always be a moment of joy for the lovers, that orgasms are always "fun," and that smiles and happy endings accompany great sex.

On the contrary, sexual climaxes can be ruthless, one-sided, opportunistic, and fearfully depressing—yet indisputably erotic at the same time. Perhaps the first thing to understand about "writing orgasms" is that describing intense arousal can appear in any and every facet of your character's emotional spectrum. When you write an ugly sex scene, its power comes from the fact that it is both ugly and erotic, just as a joyful romantic sex scene derives its power from the occasion when the erotic fuel intensifies the bliss.

Whatever its color, sexual ecstasy is a powerful experience, and at least a momentary flight to the unconscious. It's that departure from the ordinary—the disappearing act of the sexual unconscious—that is so intimidating for writers to articulate. Orgasm is famously called *la petite mort* ("the little death"), and writing the orgasm is much like writing a death scene, where characters teeter between the world as we know it and the mystery beyond.

What Does Orgasm Look Like?

What do we look like when we come? One of the difficult parts of writing about sex is that the subject is so visually taboo. Many writers only hazard guesses at what the orgasmic body looks like. Anyone who's watched the Olympics on TV could make a better stab at writing a sports story than most people could do when approaching their first depiction of a sex scene. Some visual and physiological education is in order, because your powers of observation are never more needed than when you describe an intimate act. You are going to have to go out of your way to get that education, because it isn't going to fall into your lap.

"Hey," you may say, "I've had plenty of orgasms, I don't need to study up to know what that feels like!"

Yes, you know how you *feel* when you're coming, but do you know what you *look* like? Do you know how your body changes when you become aroused, other than the obvious presence of wetness or stiffness?

You wouldn't dream of writing about a new location, a performance, or any physical activity without giving the reader a picture of the visual. It won't be sufficient to talk about how sex feels from the psychological interior, because a great deal of that "interior" emotion is created for the reader by the physical clues.

Let me start with my most radical proposition first—which I don't think would be radical at all, if our culture weren't so squeamish about sex. I want you to see yourself coming. You look in the mirror without blushing, don't you? You think nothing of examining your

face and appearance for the day. You take snapshots at every important occasion. Well, add this to your list of important occasions to be
documented: your sexual response cycle.

THE "SEE YOURSELF" ORGASM WRITING EXERCISE

- Borrow, buy, or rent a video recorder, and put it on a tri-
  pod in front of your bed.
- Press the play button and go to your mattress. Masturbate, or make love with your partner if you like. Forget
  the camera.
- When you're done, watch the tape of your sexual arousal.
- Look at your face, your skin color, your postures, the way
  you're breathing, the way the light hits you. Listen to
  yourself, listen to the bed and the floor, or listen to the
  hum of your vibrator, for that matter.
- Take notes. Write a short scene where you mix your
  physical description with the thoughts that might have
  been on your mind at the time of your arousal.
- You can erase your tape now, or treasure it forever, but
  you have just learned something very basic about yourself
  that will give you a remarkable key to sexual observation.

Goal

- To observe authentic sexual response, without cinematic
  puffery.
- To describe orgasm based on observation rather than
  memory or conjecture.
- To develop a consciousness of what sex looks like, in the
  same sense that you know what eating looks like, what
  sleep looks like, etc.

After You Finish This Exercise, You'll Never Believe Again . . .
- That Hollywood movies portray realistic sexual scenes.
- That if you've seen one orgasm, you've seen them all.

Special Note for the Dreadfully Shy: If you can't bring yourself to record your own face and body in arousal, get a copy of *The Faces of Orgasm* video by Joani Blank, available from Good Vibrations. It's a movie of many ordinary people's faces while they're having an orgasm. Nothing else. You may be so surprised that you decide to get out the video camera after all, but either way, you can continue with the observation and writing notes.

THE ORGASM MEMORY EXERCISE

There's another picture you need to capture, and this is one that requires no equipment at all. You need to articulate the images that cross your mind when you are close to orgasm. It's too bad we can't videotape our brains for those intense moments, but, instead, you're going to have to begin this process by prompting yourself to "remember what you see," as if giving yourself the autosuggestion to remember your dreams.

Most of us don't fantasize in a linear manner, with rational dialogue, characters, and logical sequencing. Our most familiar erotic thoughts are so intuitive that the images and words that cross our minds at the moment of orgasm are like touchstones, little magnets that we only attach ourselves to briefly.

When you take notes on your fantasies, don't try to "write a story" (you'll do that later!)—just write notes on your stream of consciousness, as the fantasy appears to you.

- For this exercise, I would recommend you be alone— masturbation only. Anyone else's presence is going to distract from the privacy and continuity of your fantasy process. While that might be entertaining, you want complete concentration.
- Start masturbating with no other thought than that you want to get off, and you want to think about the things that reliably arouse you.
- If you are having trouble, imagine that you want to be sexually aroused but you can't for some reason. Then, based on everything you know about your sexuality, think of a fantasy that would most likely make you aroused.
- Have a pen and paper next to you.
- Shortly after you feel satisfied, write down your answers to the following questions.

    (I've adapted these questions from the sexual-fantasy questionnaire in Jack Morin's book *The Erotic Mind*, which was written for psychological insight into the origins of our sexual fantasies but which has tremendous insights for any writer as well.)

Who is in the fantasy?
What is the location, where are you?
What do the other people look or sound like?
Are you having sex in the fantasy, or are you watching others?
What are the elements that make this fantasy so exciting?
What is the most intense point of excitement in the fantasy?
What are the feelings going on during the fantasy (joy, contentment, love, anxiety, fear, guilt, anger, jealousy, pride, relaxation, tenderness, remorse, naughtiness, revenge)?

- The first time you do this exercise, you might realize that you have easy recall for the first question, but not the second—and only partially the third, etc. That's why you'll need to do this again, and again—gosh, you might have to devote a weekend to this—until you have observed every bit of it.

- These kinds of exercises have an element of self-revelation far beyond the craft of writing. You will benefit from this process sexually, emotionally, and artistically. But with a writerly goal in mind, you can do this exercise for no other reason than that you want to be the greatest erotic storyteller the world has ever known.

Goal

- To become aware of the arc of arousal.
- To materialize the similarities between fantasy development and fiction development.
- To see the suspense and surrender of arousal from both the lover's and the writer's standpoint.

After You Finish This Exercise, You'll Never Believe Again . . .

- That sexual fantasy can, or should be, free of tension-making elements.
- That any sexual fantasy doesn't have an author's point of view.
- That the details of your fantasies are too vague, too boring, or too predictable to teach you anything new.

Somebody Else's Orgasm

Now, of course, you might say, "My body and my fantasies are unique. How are my observations going to help me write anything other than my own masturbatory memoir?"

Well, first of all, you're not so unique—in the physiological sense at least. A lot of clues about human sexual response can be seen in your body as well as everyone else's. And it's important to see those responses in a nonporno environment, where the body is not "putting on" a performance.

More important, though, is that this kind of self-observation is going to increase your empathetic eye considerably. Of course, not everyone fantasizes about convents, or German shepherds, or pop stars, but if you understand the way your fantasy grows in your unconscious, you will be much more in tune with how it could work for any of your characters.

Your Visual Erotic Education

Certainly, a simultaneous part of your education should involve looking at books, pictures, and movies of other lovers throughout history. You need to see examples of different lovers, as well as reading about them, to inspire your character development, as well as get an idea of the variety of sexual expression.

I would recommend illustrations of sexual/reproductive anatomy, as well as erotic/pornographic picture books and videos. Get a variety of things—something from ancient Japan, a *Hustler* magazine, something gay and Roman, something blue and burlesque.

One difficulty with porn is that men are usually not shown "getting hard"; they generally appear fully erect from the get-go. One video that shows men's genitals in many stages of arousal is called

Fire on the Mountain, which is actually a teaching tape about how to arouse men with your hands in a dozen different ways.

It's very New Age in its sensibility; after I watched it with my lover, we made jokes like "Let me show you the Heavenly Rainbow Stroke with Five Happiness Forefingers," as if we were reading a Chinese takeout menu. But the information in the video is extraordinary; aside from learning more about cocks than I ever thought possible, I was haunted by the tape as a writer, because it showed me so many intimate images that I really hadn't noticed before as a lover.

I Am My Lover and *Femalia* are excellent picture books about women's genitals and sexual responses, in authentic settings and with a great variety of female subjects. You also can't help but be educated by Suzanne Gage's one-of-a-kind anatomical drawings of male and female genitals in the book *New View of a Woman's Body.* She was the first to make detailed diagrams of how our genitals look and change during orgasm.

Just because you may have made love to many men or women, this doesn't mean you've seen it all. Being a participant is very different from being an observer. You must think of your education like that of a figurative painter, drawing sketches from a live model—there is no substitute for that practice. It is not something you can do simply from memory.

Your observation and your notes are going to form the basis for your best erotic writing. With your own research in mind, go back to some of your favorite erotic books—or just leaf through any volume of *The Best American Erotica,* and start noticing the physical detail and interior descriptions that accompany the orgasm scenes. With your own reportage in hand, you will see with new eyes how these writers you admire have "built" their climaxes. You will see how they've dovetailed all the details that probably came from their own observations with the trimmings and plot details provided by their imaginations.

What *Not* to Do When Writing a Big Sex Scene

I always hesitate to say "never" in writing, because it's always possible to take the worst writing habit and turn it into a fetishistic masterpiece. So when I take the risk of telling you what practices you should avoid, please understand that these are general suggestions of how to save your erotica from the most common pitfalls.

• Love Scenes Are Not Operating Instructions
Don't turn love scenes into play-by-play diagrams.

For example, don't write:

"Marcy draped her left arm over Doug's shoulder as her right hand reached for his belt buckle."

Just how many hands does Marcy have? Two, that's correct; and unless there is some compelling reason to know why Marcy is using her left or right appendages, I don't want to hear about it. Instead, try:

"Marcy draped one arm over Doug's shoulder as her other hand reached for his belt buckle."

That brings us visually to concentrate on Marcy's aggressiveness and Doug's undoing, rather than stopping to contemplate the direction of Marcy's limbs.

Erotic scenes are acts of passion. You don't want to reduce body parts to a running diagram of measurements and traffic signals:

"Licking my way three inches up her left knee, I felt her ejaculate splatter my right cheek."

This unerotic attention to the wrong details is what is known as "mechanical" sex writing, and you want to rid yourself of the neurosis at its first showing. Yes, there's always the chance that you might get swept away and accidentally describe something that is physically impossible, or that makes a break in continuity, but you can clarify that later in your editing process.

- Ooo! Eeee! Ooo-Ah-Ah!

Don't use sex noises to substitute for description.

Sexual sounds—the moans, gasps, and shouts of inhibition falling to the wayside—are some of the most erotic aspects of making love. To *listen* to such noises can be very arousing, without any other filler necessary. However, to *read* about a groan or a sigh is something else altogether. You cannot write an orgasm scene successfully by merely transcribing the sounds one can hear through a thin wall.

Here's an example of a weakly written sex passage that relies on aural transcription alone:

"OOOOhh," Cary moaned. "Oh god, ahhhh, owwwwwww, baby, oh oh oh oh, gahhhhhhh, aieee, oooooohhhh, yeahhhhhhh, yeah-hhh!"

Sorry, but if I knew what Cary was doing, and what she looked like when she was vocalizing, her orgasm scene would be a lot hotter. It's even better to have some dialogue that gives a hint, at least, of what's going on in the character's mind:

"Oh God," Cary moaned, twisting her fingers inside her cunt, facedown, cream trailing down her thighs, her pillow sopping wet from stifling her cries. "Don't—please, don't do it." She shuddered—and bearing down with her hips, she crushed the pillows beneath her.

Here we get the idea that Cary is making a lot of noise, even though most of the words are not "sound effects." But we also see her voicing these words, and we get an idea of some thought that's torturing her or inspiring her excitement. We have a lot more information to make an arousing character.

Actually, my first attempt at Cary's screaming is better than that of many of the vocalizing sinners I come across who try to create their own orgasmic language and spelling from scratch:

"Aiieeooooooo!!!!!" Cary shrieked. "Maaahhhheeeeeeeoooooooo!!!!!! Unnngghhh!"

When I see that many exclamation marks, I smell a stink bomb.

It's humorous at best, but not erotic. When writers go crazy with nutty punctuation and made-up sound effects, I know they are striving for something that would be much better portrayed with a few strong verbs and some adequate description. Think of strong vocabulary that describes action well and also looks sexy on the page; that's where your orgasmic language will take place.

- Fuck It Fuck It Fuck It

Don't make curses and epithets do all the work for you.

Lovers who curse at the moment of truth are a bona fide phenomenon. But once again, like sound effects, you can't make swear words do all the dirty work for you. They have a nice shock effect, but you'll wear them out in a paragraph or two if you aren't as considerate with them as you would be with any vocabulary.

Swearing in print eloquently takes two talents. One is an ear for how people curse in their uninhibited speech. I'm sure there are lots of good examples, but for a writer who excels in dialogue, punctuated with continuous curses, my favorite is playwright David Mamet. He has an incredible ear for how the seemingly inarticulate can speak volumes. Read a couple of his contemporary plays out loud and you're already halfway there to understanding the art of raging speech.

Second, as noted above, no matter how tight your dialogue, you need enough description, character, and scene setting so that we can see the context in which these ecstatic monologues take place.

- After the Deluge

Don't end your sex scene without a postorgasmic reflection.

After the peak of your orgasm, you have no place to come but down; as a writer, you must navigate *down* that cliff as perceptively as you moved up. You can't just yell "Heigh-ho, Silver!" and then fall off your horse. Don't cop out on sexual endings; they require grace and attention, as well as an eye to where the story is going next.

Don't turn postorgasmic scenes into commercials where you demonstrate what lovers should do in the moments following climax. Instead, make it a moment where your characters reveal something essential about themselves; then the plot moves forward.

The movie cliché about postcoitus is where we see the lovers light up their cigarettes. In novel writing, the equivalent chestnut is to have the lovers fluff up their pillows and deliver some profound message to each other, the moral lesson of the tale. Ugh! Yes, if you have characters who can never let a quiet moment go by without some pompous pronouncement, then by all means have them give an arrogant sermon in their orgasmic aftermath.

But in most cases, the moments following climax are noted for the small actions and gestures that speak volumes, the words that indicate states of mind, and a return to self-consciousness. Let your sex scene exhale, and draw a complete breath before you start running again.

Sex and Violence

Censoring sexual material in the Victorian age was pretty straightforward. A minister called attention to some bit of writing or art that he deemed obscene. The offending object was either banned or redone to remove its sexually provocative aspect.

No one ever asked, "Is this sex good or bad?" It didn't matter if it was noble or debased, educational or prurient. *Any* kind of sexual expression was considered immoral.

However, since the heyday of Victorian repression, we've had several artistic and political revolutions. There are standards for "obscenity" that exempt any material with artistic, social, or educational value. Most people agree today that in *some* kind of context, sexual discussion is appropriate.

Our more liberal laws and climate have certainly loosened up the restrictions around Herotica, but they've also created new ones. The common way to repress sexuality today is not to say it's simply sexual but to say that it is sexual and *violent*.

This magic phrase, "sex and violence," has been used to condemn everything from blow-job porn videos to works of art at the Smithsonian. It is used to imply perversion and evil intent, regardless of the artist's original vision. It's mighty effective rhetoric, but it's incomprehensible as description, since no one agrees on what "sex and violence" looks like, or if there's ever any reason to depict it.

Writers face a painful experience when a single aspect of their work is exploited by the "sex and violence" canard. Suddenly, the original purpose is lost; the style and context no longer have any room to be considered. The object of the uninvited attention—the author's story—becomes so fetishized as to be unrecognizable.

This chapter is about two things—first, how to cope with a defaming attack on your work that uses "sex and violence" as its pitchfork; and second, how to address themes of sexuality and violence from a writer's perspective. The two problems have little in common because the first is a political game and the second is about a writer's personal perspective.

The People Who Want to Shut You Up

Unfortunate fact of life: There are people who don't like sexual expression. You won't always understand what makes them tick—and, believe me, they don't either. Perhaps they are elitists or opportunists. Maybe they're religious zealots or bigots. Whatever their motives, they decide to go after sexual content and beat it back with a stick.

Whatever their reasons, the would-be censors know they will have no success if they attack sexuality on its face—they would be accused of subverting the Constitution, of being prudes, or of functioning as the social-control fanatics they actually are.

So instead of saying "Sex is bad," they say "Violence and sex are bad." This is such an obvious claim that there's no intelligent argument against it, except to say that the statement itself is disingenuous. No one in their right mind is pro-murder, or a rape supporter. So these advocates must have something else in mind, something particular that is more controversial, and it would be more honest of them to come out and say what that is.

Sex and violence, on the face of it, sounds like an assault. But do writers become murderers or rapists when they treat these themes in their work? Should every cruel act described in writing be taken in the same context?

Modern-day censors typically proclaim that certain kinds of sexual speech are bad for children, or for old people, or for prisoners, or for the disabled, or for people in military service. Any weakened or captive group will do—the more disenfranchised, the better. The censors appeal to the majority population to "protect" this group of "vulnerable" individuals, even if it has to be at the expense of what could presumably be expressed to educated, mature adults.

If you've been following the news in recent years of what has happened to the arts, the music world, and the movie and publishing trades, you can easily take my quick formula for censorship and fill in the specifics. The NEA has been nearly gutted because of fears about sexuality. Rebellious music—the "Frankie and Johnnie" lyrics of our era—has been attacked because of its sexuality. The movie rating system has come apart at the seams because its values about sexuality are so out of step with what most filmmakers want to say.

So what does all this mean to you, as one writer who wants to create the very best erotica and storytelling that you can?

Your Secret Jargon Decoder Ring

First, you have to turn your secret jargon decoder ring to "high." When someone brings up the question of "violence" in your work, or argues that your work is "harmful," you need to understand that this is a political question, not a literary one. You need to set your interrogators straight with some perceptive undermining of their rhetoric. Many times you will find that what they object to is not "violence," per se, but rather homosexuality, group sex, vaginal or anal penetration, sex outside of marriage, sex toys, etc.—a lot of *non*violent activities that nevertheless may inflame viewers because of their religious or political opinions.

Define "Violence"

Here are five definitions of what "violence" is, according to my Merriam-Webster dictionary:

1. Exertion of physical force so as to injure or abuse.
2. Injury by or as if by infringement or profanation.
3. Intense or furious, often destructive action or force.
4. Vehement, extreme feeling or expression; intensity.
5. Jarring quality: discordance.

Now try to imagine literature, or any art, without those qualities. It would be dead. There would be no weather, no passion, no convergence. Violence is not merely a fetish or an object, it is a natural phenomenon. It is an inherent dynamic of all tragedy, and much of comedy as well.

In any given story, warriors may be praised or damned, hurricanes may be viewed in awe or grief, social disruption can be transcendent or ruinous. Some violent acts in literature, such as murder or rape, are traditionally treated as damnable, but that doesn't mean that they disappear or are undescribed. In fact, their very description is often part of the author's message and sensitivity on the subject.

Sex can include violent qualities or violent actions—for good or for evil, or for further existential contemplation. These elements might create erotic tension or sexual ambivalence in the reader. That is probably the most sensitive aspect of violence in literature: that it could simultaneously horrify and arouse us. When sexual tension is conflated with bad deeds, however, this is not an invention of literature, it's a graphic observation of life's real tortures and madness. Authors will address the human conundrum of pleasure and pain as long as we have a way to express ourselves, and sometimes it will be profound, and other times it will be crap.

There is no point in a discussion about whether erotic literature should include violence, because to exempt sexuality, or violence, from the range of normal human experience is to pretend as if these two things exist outside of us, instead of within. We all know how life is, we know its ups and downs, its contented moments and its extremes. Writers should never be troubled by accusations that their work is "dangerous"—the greater danger is gratuitous pandering.

Self-Censorship

Erotic writers face three common threats from the "violence" theme. The first, which only you can evaluate, is your own sense of authenticity and confidence in your work. If you start hiding ideas in your work before anyone even gets a chance to look at it, you've stabbed yourself in the back. You must never anticipate or calculate what will be "acceptable" in your own back room—not unless you're striving for a career of mediocrity.

Publisher's Restrictions

As a professional writer, you may encounter publishers at every level of the food chain who have content "rules" for what they will or won't publish. You must understand that these rules are the self-imposed restraints that publishers have made; they're often independent of what is legal, let alone artistically relevant.

Here's what is outlawed in American writing: *nothing*. You can't say that about every country, or every year in U.S. history, but thanks to a battle fought by many artists and activists, we have absolute protection when it comes to freedom of speech.

Note that this is not true about pictures—only words. It is currently illegal to publish photographs of naked children (under eighteen, as defined by the law), even if the intent is not prurient. There is a lot of legal and artistic debate about this legislation—because, as you can imagine, it has caused a great deal of harm to people who take cute photos of their kids in plastic swimming pools, or to artists and educators who portray nudity as a natural part of life at all ages.

But I don't want to go into the pictorial question for the moment. All you need to know as an author is that you can *write* about anything, with absolute certainty that it is legally protected speech, and that no one can prosecute you for writing anything, short of libel and slander.

However, publishers can decide that they want to disallow a certain kind of content, simply because their presses are their babies. They can decide "No sex between gay men," or "No sexual fantasies from underage characters," or "No S/M"—it's all their personal whim, not a matter of legality. They may be selling to stores that have prohibitive standards, or they may be exporting to countries that have more stringent rules. Their desire to make as much money as possible is typically what drives them to push for the lowest acceptable denominator.

Also, some publishers believe they will be the object of nuisance lawsuits if they publish controversial material. The persecution may be frivolous; nevertheless, it will cost them money that they don't have. I've noticed that gay erotica publishers have more content rules then anyone, because they are the most threatened by legal actions, however dubious.

If a publisher has a list of verboten topics, it needs to tell you up front. Then, rather than argue the merits of its decisions, you have to decide whether it's worth it to you to write for it. Do not be intimidated by its boundaries, but simply decide whether they give you enough room to write well and if the compensation the publisher is offering is worth the unnatural limitations.

Advertisers Judge Your Story

Writing professionally nearly always means writing with limits. Magazines are the worst, because they will do practically anything to appease their advertisers. Some ad exec at Ford or Procter & Gamble might think your work is too sexy or too controversial, and—*BING!*—it's killed. I once had a story killed by someone at Hanes Hosiery—I wonder what they're up to today.

Making an Example of One Book

Book publishers tend to be more liberal, although they may have an image they want to preserve. They don't want to be boycotted or reviled by every media pundit in the country. They don't want the heat—unless it translates into revenue. Sometimes a work will become objectified as "a bad thing," like Bret Easton Ellis's *American Psycho*. Ellis's book was an extraordinary case because it was contracted to one publisher, who then pulled the book after it was ready to go on sale. Why? Because some colleagues close to the publisher and the media read review copies and denounced it as violent and degrading to women.

Now, was *American Psycho* the most shocking, controversial book ever published? Of course not! Not a single person has ever died from reading it, nor would you be able to find a consensus among critics who reviewed it. It concerns a wealthy Manhattan playboy whose excesses and obsessions include murder, but it's hardly a prescription for his lifestyle—vicious satire is more like it.

However, someone powerful was offended by the book, or at least offended by the author, and decided to make an example of him. This person decided to create a bogeyman—that *American Psycho* was dangerous to the public and that Ellis's writing it was tantamount to an act of terrorism. But then, of course, another publisher picked up the title, and it was released without much further ado.

American Psycho is noteworthy because it's a rather rare case for a major publisher to reject a book by one of its stars. It will be remembered by authors for a long time because of its chilling effect. Every book writer has the insecurity, "What if they throw this one out?"—and legends like the case of *American Psycho* add to their anxiety. Yes, it was a publicity bonanza, but many readers, especially women, never read the book because they believed it was a belligerent attack against them. No writer enjoys that kind of villainy.

The reason books are not considered "dangerous" more often is because reading is not nearly as in vogue as it used to be. Movies and music are the current whipping boys of political opportunism, and that's because they're so much more popular than books.

Your Fans' Reaction

Finally, there's your readers—those with whom you are familiar, and those you've never met. If you portray your subjects authentically, and there are troubling passages in your story, then you will inevitably get under your readers' skin—and there's no point in anticipating it if you want to preserve your creative mind.

Here's the rub: Writing is ultimately exhibitionist. People see your naked imagination at work, and they may be shocked to see what you "look" like in the buff. At the same time, we authors get a good deal of pleasure from "exposing" ourselves, because we know that the power of our work is proven when we make others react so strongly.

How to Protect Yourself from Censorship's Slings and Arrows

Censorship, from either your own fears or the world at large, is always going to be poking its nose in your business. The first key to keeping your sanity is never to take accusations of "harm" or "violence" to heart. The people who use those words are bullies and cowards—they have nothing to do with your creative process.

If you're a professional writer, make sure you have a variety of places where you write—including your own projects/diaries/letters, which are uncompromised by anyone.

Always begin by writing without constraint. You, or a publisher, can edit for their "rules" later.

I write for some publications that don't allow certain "naughty" words. I write for publishers that have a very unsophisticated idea of what can be said about sex. But I also write for many outlets where I can speak my mind, and I can let my characters speak as they please. I self-publish on my Web page, where I'm the only one making the rules. I write privately, for no one but myself or a dear friend.

Keep a long-term point of view, because you have a lifetime of writing ahead of you. Use discretion to protect your private life without apologies.

I've refrained from some nonfiction material out of concern for my family, but I've expressed identical emotional truths in my fiction. I know in twenty years I'll be able to write about certain things that I can't even get a handle on now, and I look forward to it. And although I haven't used a pseudonym in ages, if I had a compelling reason to use one, I wouldn't feel guilty—I'd be happy to get the work out there, and to protect whoever was on my mind.

Remember, censorship is just a legal term for lying. But we don't have to pander to its proponents and apologists. It may be a very big, very socially acceptable method of lying, but it is still nothing but a charade. As an observer of life, you know when the emperor wears no clothes; as a writer, you must report and judge that naked state of affairs as you see fit.

How to Think About Violence in Your Own Work

Working with violent and tragic material in a story is part of classic drama, and any writer who works with these themes is striving for authenticity and a wide range of emotional response. About the only thing that's as awkward as a forced romantic or erotic moment is a tragic description that comes across as phony or banal. Perhaps this is the real reason " sex" and "violence" have so often been singled out by critics—they're both so tough to write with grace and sensitivity. Scenes of pain, shock, and distress are most effective when you write "softly" yet carry a big emotional stick. Throwing around special effects, like curses and buckets of blood, won't impact your reader if they are predictable, or if they substitute for character development.

VIOLENCE EXERCISE

Let's spend some time investigating and interpreting your own personal experiences with violence.

- Give yourself two or three minutes to write a response to each of the following questions. Set a timer for each one; when the time is up, stop in your tracks and move on to the next question.
- What is the most violent act that has ever happened personally to your body?
- What is the most violent act you've ever witnessed in person?
- What is the most violent act you've ever heard, watched,

or read about, real or imagined—in books, movies, on radio or TV, or by word of mouth?

- What's the most violent thing you've ever done to another person?

Take a break, and then read your responses out loud. If you have a partner or group to share these answers with, so much the better.

Write a short essay addressing the following questions about your memories of violent acts:

- What kind of weight do you give your experiences in each of the above categories? Which kind of violence was the most grave, the most memorable?
- Does one or another play a bigger part in your memory or behavior?
- Do some acts seem like trifles and others more dangerous?
- Do you think that any of the violence, or your reaction to it, was justified?
- Is there a sexual or erotically arousing component to any of the scenes you described?

Experimental Writing

"**Experimental writing**" **is** a term that begs the question "Just what is it, anyway?" So many parodies are associated with "experimental genius": everything from Frankenstein to a botched cooking project—or the merry narcissist in a black leotard, dancing to her own private poetry.

To say that one is an "experimental writer" often invites nothing but ridicule and incomprehension. Many people assume that if it's not traditional work, it must be self-indulgent rot. But some of my favorite writers whom I've published in *The Best American Erotica* series are deliberately experimental in their contributions: Robert Gluck, Camille Roy, Linda Smukler, Dodie Bellamy, Bob Flanagan, Kevin Killian, Greg Boyd, Michelle Tea, and Bart Plantenga.

Everything in art and literature that is *now* called traditional, or mainstream, was once thought of as experimental. Once upon time, novels were experimental. All the popular reading phenomena that can be found at an airport bookstore today were once fueled by authors who took risks, who tried something that "nobody" understood. But those "nobodies" have, on occasion, turned the literary mainstream upside down. When writers ask me if they should write in a nontraditional manner, I want to offer them all the inspiration I can—because frankly, I'm counting on them to break the mold.

Experimental forms are put down for only one reason—because they are not seen as commercially viable. In fact, one could make an excellent case that the avant-garde crosses over into the status quo the minute it makes a buck for itself. Is that betrayal or wild success? This question of when the fringe becomes the fabric is the source of 90 percent of the friction between the haves and have-nots of the writing world.

Nevertheless, when I look back on my own history as a writer and performer, my most thrilling efforts—and perhaps the ones least publicly appreciated—were when I was doing something that my peers considered completely off the wall.

My "experimental" career started when I was nineteen and got it into my head that I wanted to join an improvisational theater group. I had never had "regular" theater training before; when I heard that I had to audition with a monologue to get into the "experimental" group, I was bewildered. I barely knew what a monologue was, and I didn't have time to do much research in the twenty-four hours we had to prepare. If it was "improv," I wondered, why did we have to memorize and deliver a prepared subject? But I still wanted to get in.

I went home to look at all my books, and I saw that my "black power" section included a book called *Black Drama Anthology*—a collection of radical plays by authors like LeRoi Jones (Amiri Baraka), who probably was the reason I bought the book to begin with. Among all the plays in the collection, I was especially attracted to a great speech by a fiery woman character, and I decided I could memorize that. Would anyone think it was weird that I was a stringy-haired white girl reading the part of an old black woman? Oh, well, it was too late to find anything else.

There were a lot of dropped jaws at the audition when I stood up to deliver my ghetto soliloquy. I had no idea whether they thought I was crazy or the most daring prodigy they'd ever seen, so I just prayed that I could remember my speech from the first word to the last. The last time I had memorized anything was lengthy prayers in Catholic school, but that came in handy—I got through my monologue without a blank spot.

Who knows why they picked me—I have a feeling that the

troupe needed a fifth female. What I did find out, from the first day we worked together, was that I was going to learn how to write scripts through improvisation—and that this process, in which the oddest catalysts would lead us to deeply revealing scenes, was the most imaginative work I'd ever done. I loved it.

In addition to theater and "performance art" (as experimental theater came to be called in the 1970s), I was inspired by many California poets of the 1950s and 1960s—their rebellious politics, their unabashed sexuality, and their insistence that your art could transport you to an entirely new level of consciousness.

I had a lover at this time who was trying to craft the perfect Top 40 pop song; he thought my poetry/performance work was completely whacked. I got hotter about my improv group and cooler about him. I vowed that I would rather die than take my stage training and go to Hollywood to get a Burger King commercial or a soap opera role.

I decided to move to San Francisco. I'd heard of audiences there who welcomed experimental performance works and poetry readings; I'd heard of an alternative art movement that was the opposite of everything Los Angeles had to offer at the time.

The rumors were true. I cowrote and directed a play called *Girls Gone Bad* at the theater Project Artaud; it was the first sexual work I ever produced, long before *On Our Backs* magazine or the *Herotica* anthologies. *Girls Gone Bad* was my first attempt at articulating female erotic rebellion The entire show was created through improvisation and reinterpretations of pulp novels.

In the wake of my performance success, a poet named Myrna Elana wrote to me that she was starting a "lesbian sex magazine" and that she was eager to publish my poetry. This is the poem I gave her, which was my first published erotic work:

The One About Debbie
curled like an angel in my pocket
like a flashy lucky charm   slipped down a crack

THESE are soda cracker memories
I crush them in my hands
I never missed you so much
as when you resurfaced
climbing off that wave like Venus on a saltine
it lingers in my mouth
and there, it stings my fingers

The whole notion of lesbian-made erotica was definitely "experimental." As I began to spend most of my time working on the *On Our Backs* debut, I was confronted by booksellers, distributors, printers, media, and plenty of critical readers who said that the entire notion of "lesbian sex" sounded like an oxymoron. The popular wisdom was that women, especially lesbians—and especially feminists—were passionless, except for political causes. We wouldn't be able to eroticize our way out of a paper bag, according to the experts. But our first issue was a strong rebuke to that stereotype; we received everything from flowers on our doorstep to calls for our assassination.

When I created *Herotica*, a collection of diverse erotic stories by women authors, in 1987, my publisher and I were met with skepticism and anger by everyone in the publishing business, not just the lesbian side. Big publishers said that women would only read romances, not erotica. Period. Feminist presses thought we were giving the cause a bad name by focusing on female sexual pleasure.

I'd grown accustomed to what it was like to be a threat—I could judge my effectiveness by the waterline of controversy. This time it was really high. I knew that all the critics and nay-sayers were in tremendous denial about women's authentic sexual interest and how empowering it could be.

Today, you'd be hard-pressed to find anyone who considers "women's erotica" to be avant-garde or shocking. This just goes to show how quickly something can move from the margins to the thick of pop culture when the timing is right. I try to imagine what it must have been like for Allen Ginsberg and his publisher, Lawrence Ferlinghetti, to publish *Howl* in 1956—and to suddenly find their whole movement, the dropouts of America, in the middle of *Time* magazine. No one undertakes these experiments with the plan to create an anthem for a pent-up generation, but that's exactly what can happen.

Your Very Own Experiment

You'll never be able to define experimental literature except to say that it's new territory for your writing, and perhaps it's something that no one else will understand. Maybe even *you* don't understand it, but you're compelled to follow your Pied Piper nonetheless. Your compulsion is what counts. Forget understanding your process, forget trying to explain why you're doing it.

Dump the arguments and speeches about why this "might work." What's so wonderful about experiments is that often they *don't* work. They *do* blow up in the oven; the Bride of Frankenstein *does* crawl out and strangle you with a black leotard while you shout your last prayers. It's only once you've tasted your own shocking failures, harebrained ideas, and sudden departures that you will realize something quite wonderful.

Experimental Excursions

A writing experiment for any author is to reach for the unfamiliar. I'm not going to tell you to climb under a table, or write an essay in three-letter words, or begin your novel on LSD—because if you're interested in experimental prose, chances are you've already been there and done that. Experimentation is the ultimate exercise in exploding your own boundaries, not living up to someone else's outlandish stereotypes.

I will offer two general inspirations, though: poetry and theater. These two will introduce you to a world of variation from traditional narrative writing. Immerse yourself; take a vacation from your normal genres. Why not write a song today, instead of a chapter? Take one of your stories, and write it completely in dialogue, as if performed on stage. Pick a Mother Goose rhyme and redo it as erotic verse. Read a book of haiku and make your own erotic versions in the same meter.

Consider experimental writing as your first escape from burnout. Don't worry about what defines experimental—consider it anything that YOU don't usually do. It's your holiday from your familiar pets and formulas; it's your invitation to a risk.

Experimentation comes more easily when you are in a milieu that is excited by it. Create a compatible writers' group that provides a place where you can goad each other on to be adventurous, to take a trip where no one knows the destination.

How to Mix Sex with Other Genres:
Sci-fi, Horror, Crime, Romance

The most righteous trend in erotic writing today is, in many cases, that no one is calling it "erotica." Sex has regained its rightful place in the heart of all literature. Sure, there will always be a place for the dirty joke, the bawdy story, the novella of sexual obsession—but "erotic" writing, at its most creative and organic, is something that takes place naturally in all varieties of storytelling. Today, old classics are being released unexpurgated, and new writers are no longer ghettoizing their sexual work—the combination of old and new creative liberty has been intoxicating.

The Hundred-Year-Old Revolution

The most outstanding erotic work being published today is not some new hot imprint, or a precocious new author—it is the unexpurgated reprints of books that have been abused, buried, and sanitized for over a century.

Two hundred years after he wrote his infamous memoirs, that wonderful writer and lover Casanova finally had his twelve-volume autobiography published (in 1997) in its original uncensored version. Casanova isn't the only one getting a new lease on his literary life. Scholars, publishers, and readers are part of a tidal wave of contemporary interest in uncovering the "real" deal on classic works of literature that have been bastardized for a hundred-plus years. The cork is out of the bottle.

How did the world's greatest literature get so screwed, and why are we just beginning to make amends? It's hard to fathom that a few blowhards in nineteenth-century Victorian England managed to mangle the entire globe's literature for so many generations. But that's exactly what happened. The very word *bowdlerize*, which means to remove the sexual content of any piece of work, comes from Dr. Thomas Bowdler, a prominent literary fixture in Victorian England. At England's colonial peak, Bowdler succeeded in rewriting every one of Shakespeare's plays with all the "dirty" parts taken out.

Destroying Shakespeare was Bowdler's most notorious attack on the English language, but he also succeeded in demolishing many other great works of his own era. In each case, the original author's work was made unrecognizable by "Bowdlerized" versions that took every hint of naughtiness out and replaced them with something a Puritan could stomach.

Yet Bowdler, as one person, can't be blamed for everything. He only rewrote Shakespeare; the expurgation of other literary works was the work of others, in the repressive spirit of the times. England's political power was so dominant in Europe, and throughout the world, that the movement to "clean up" work in the English language extended to everywhere Britannia ruled the waves.

The Dream of the Red Chamber, an epic eighteenth-century Chinese novel of several generations in a prominent family, had all the sex taken out. The same with *Arabian Nights,* the Greek myths, the Roman histories. Face it, virtually every great (dramatic) classic prior to the Victorian age has some kind of sex in it, and the puritans took out every bit of it. The only way you could read the original, uncensored texts was to have elite scholarly knowledge and highly privileged access to the unexpurgated work.

The puritan values of Victorian England no longer rule, but they are still the most visible of all our cultural attitudes about sexuality.

By contrast, intellectual and artistic movements since the beginning of the twentieth century have wanted nothing to with those old religious and superstitious trappings. But change has come slowly, and the erotic renaissance is still working its way back into popular modern literature.

The "Manly" Genres

It's no surprise to see that literature for the fairer sex has always had a patronizing attitude toward women and sexuality. But what about genres that were originally pitched to men: sci-fi, horror, true crime?

Science Fiction

Of course this type of fiction has plenty of female fans today, but when it first came out, in the early days of paperback publishing, sci-fi was considered a taste for masculine interest only. Like the crime, horror, and western genres, sci-fi flourished in pulp magazines for years before paperback books started up.

Science fiction was revolutionary in terms of its visionary futurist projections, but until Kurt Vonnegut came along—not to mention J. G. Ballard—the sci-fi attitude toward sex was adolescent, like much of its audience: big on technology, squeamish about human contact. Not surprisingly, Vonnegut and Ballard, along with other sophisticated sci-fi writers, soon became understood as "literary" authors, and were not identified with the strict sci-fi tag anymore. Today writers like William Gibson occupy the sci-fi, literary, and erotic interest categories simultaneously—and unapologetically.

In the most subversive twist of all, sci-fi television, exemplified by *Star Trek*, became the breeding ground for the enormously popular "slash" fiction, whereby an erotic relationship between characters resembling Captain Kirk and Mr. Spock is grafted onto the familiar terrain and scripts that surround both characters. When *Star Trek* or

Charlie's Angels fans create their own erotic kingdom for the characters to play in, it's the final retribution for Dr. Bowdler . . . instead of taking sex out of books already written, slash-fiction acolytes are adding sex where it never previously existed.

Crime

My latest client still hadn't told me his name. He sat upright in the Chippendale, facing me, his legs spread against the chair arms so I had a front-row seat for the action. Wearing nothing but a silk robe, he played with his asshole during our interview, watching me for a reaction. His hole, puckered and red, looked resigned to this treatment. He slid two fingers back and forth inside himself as he waited for my reply.

"Well, Mr. McCabe?" he said, not stopping his rhythm.

"I'm not sure I can help. I usually look for things of value. You can buy a dildo at any sex shop."

He stopped and sat up. His dick parted the folds of the robe, throbbing in the surrounds of silk. "It's not any dildo. It's invaluable."

"Why? Lose your virginity on it?"

He smiled languidly. "No, that might make it an antique, but hardly worth the effort."

—"The Maltese Dildo," by Adam McCabe, from *Sex Toy Tales*

The history of crime writing is where nasty, sexy violence—and I say this with relish, not disdain—makes its most outlandish display.

Everyone knows that the heroes of crime fiction are tough guys, just one step away from hell's inferno themselves. Their temptations, surrenders, and revenges are the erotic arc of their quest for justice.

My father, a great fan of paperback fiction since its earliest appearance in the 1940s, has a favorite memory of the book cover design on Mickey Spillane's most famous crime story, *I, the Jury*. The cover illustrated the denouement of the story, where Mike Hammer, the detective who never met a woman he didn't chew up and spit out, confronts his luscious girlfriend, who, he has realized, is the killer he's been hunting. In the cover picture, she's unbuttoning her blouse, the fabric pulled back just to the point where her nipples are ready to burst forth. She's taunting him with her striptease: You wouldn't hurt me now, would you?

Instead of ripping off the rest of her clothes and ravishing her on the spot (which is exactly what the reader has been aroused to imagine at this point), the detective cocks his gun and shoots her—right in the gut.

Crime fiction's erotic MO has always been to use sex as titillation, and violence as the ejaculation. The simultaneous sadism and moralism arouse us and finish us off.

Nowadays, we have writers who are experimenting with the crime genre to use sex more explicitly and to push the boundaries of how violence, retribution, and sexuality can enhance or repel each other.

Here's an excerpt from author Susanna Moore's novel *In the Cut*, where a police detective is questioning the victim of a recent attack at her home:

"Someone," I said, "left a rubber hand under my mailbox."

"When was this?"

"Last week. Tuesday. Monday."

"Why didn't you tell me?"

[. . .] He stood, the chair still startling him a little, even though he'd sat in it a few times by then. "Tell me again," he said, "what happened to you tonight. Go over it once again. Come here. Show me."

He came up behind me and pulled me back against him, my head against his shoulder. I took his right arm, bending it at the elbow, and laid it across my neck. I could feel his breath against the side of my face.

"Like this," I said. "Like this."

He let his arm fall from my neck, down across my chest, until his hand was on my breast, his fingers finding the nipple. He pulled me back against him. He had an erection. I could feel it.

Moore's scene is erotic because it blurs the line between the criminal and the crime-stopper. The ethical barrier, the standard formalities, is broken between the victim and the cop. Their interrogation dance is a ploy for seduction, and her memory of an attack has become an intimate code for sexual invitation. Both characters talk around their attraction by playing on the idea of physical threat and submission. Neither of them is the least bit helpless, but they sure seem expert in eliciting that possibility.

Horror

Horror stories have always been, at their center, compelling erotica, because they directly address our attraction to what we fear. A typical horror myth describes a body that has been distorted, a figure who expresses ugliness and transgression in their physical extreme. That tragic "monster" character sacrifices everything in a search for beauty, a miraculous embrace with the cherished and precious. Whether it's Frankenstein reaching out to touch a little girl's hand or Dracula swooning for a bite upon a virgin's neck, it's always Beauty and the Beast; it's always a search for redemption through physical contact of the most intimate kind. The wounds that monsters make upon their victims' bodies are not-so-subtle substitutes for intercourse.

Horror writers have always used kinky tricks to amplify just how horrid their villains and creatures really are. A monster is by definition perverted, and if you are daring enough as a horror writer, you will make your monster as sexy as he is creepy. Voilà—Hannibal Lecter emerges.

What's new in horror/erotica is that some authors are not so keen to glorify the pretty virgins anymore; they'd rather cultivate more sexual and perverted sympathy for the Beast. Maybe the real horror show is the "normal people," a.k.a. the Stepford Wives. The unphotogenic kinky antiheroes are the new saviors for the future, and virgins can either get with it or get out of the way.

Give Me Romance or Give Me Death

Women's romances have been the trickiest last frontier of erotic writing, and one of its most curious niches. Sure, Jacqueline Susann did her part, in *Valley of the Dolls*, to introduce vivid sex to the traditional female soap opera genre, but the women's romance market stands apart from bestselling crossover literature. Its writers have been curiously fetishistic about what they would or would not say about sexual arousal in a love story.

As Ann Snitow wrote in her essay "Mass Market Romance: Pornography for Women Is Different," romance novels were, and are, the traditional prurient reading for nice girls. They are written with every intention of stimulating the reader, from heart palpitations to orgasm. They seek to stroke the feminine fantasies of enchantment, seduction, conquest, and adventure. But they have always been very careful to make the reader feel that she was never sacrificing her virtue or her good reputation in enjoying such salacious stories. In both their moralism and their language, romance novels have centered around the triumphs of "good girls," particularly good girls who save wayward men.

The first big erotic hurdle to overcome in romance novels is the language. In the 1970s, romance writers like Rosemary Rogers, with her risqué novel *Sweet Savage Love*, were at the right time in the right place to start using more racy sex words, like *cock* instead of *pulsing member*, and *coming* instead of *spending himself*. During the following decades, we've seen a lot of explicit language about the male half of the sex act. Liberating, yes, but curiously one-sided.

It's traditionally been taboo in romance writing to describe a woman's sexual body in as much detail as a man's, as well as her sexual feelings. The word *clitoris* has been largely MIA in women's romance novels until very recently, as has any explicit description of cunnilingus, or other sex that involves women's genitals responding to direct stimulation.

Women romance readers were considered averse to reading about their own bodies, much like male porn fans were judged to be too squeamish to see a naked male body. In both cases, there's an assumption that the heterosexual fantasy will be blown to smithereens if the reader is asked to consider the body of her or his own gender in a sexual way. And in both cases, some adventurous publishers have proved both those homophobic prejudices to be wrong.

The strangest part of romance eroticism has been the emphasis on orgasmic fulfillment through no-frills, minimal foreplay, penis/vagina intercourse. Long after *The Hite Report* revealed that over 70 percent of women do not come from intercourse alone, romance novels have defied reality by having every single one of their heroines climax from the mere thrust of a man's penis into their vaginas. It sounded magnificent in all its emotion, but honestly, *Hustler* magazine had a more realistic view of the female sexual response.

Romance fans have long protested to critics that the genre is incredibly varied. They point out that many heroines are feminists, or at least independent women, strong and tough enough to pursue their own dreams. But I don't think that's new—the strongest, toughest, most proto-feminist romance heroine of all time has got to be Scarlett O'Hara, and she was created in the 1930s.

My critique of romance novels and their ambivalent attitude toward sex isn't that the women characters are clinging vines. It's that I rarely see these heroines masturbate, touch their clits, use a vibrator, or have any kind of meaningful orgasm without penis/vagina penetration. They are also maniacal on the subject of monogamy. Those themes might be arousing to some, and a badge of virtue to others, but they are definitely not the only game in town for women. As women have had access to more explicit erotic literature, not to mention videos, they've been either abandoning the romance genre or seeking new romance writers who are hip enough to tolerate some deviations in emotions and erotic activity. This is where best-sellers like *Sex and the City* have found their mark—books with characters who talk about how real women come, and show some sexual variety.

Even as I write this chapter, romance novels are where the fastest and most unexpected erotic innovation is taking place. A huge commercial breakthrough came with the success of romance writer Robin Schone, whose novel *The Lady's Tutor* revealed the clitoris and devoted itself to the details of women's rapture and arousal. The heroine did unladylike acts, with her rump in the air, while still managing to be noble, brave, and true.

In Schone's short story "A Lady's Pleasure," from a romance collection called *Captivated*, the author shows her heroine taking a sexually assertive and daring role:

Robert had never realized how deeply a woman's tongue could penetrate a man's desires. He fisted his hand in the warm curtain of her hair and took control of the kiss.

Only to find that when he dueled her tongue back into her mouth, she sucked on his like he had earlier sucked on hers until she hung from him like a groan.

"What else, Robert?" Her breath was a whisper of heat on his lips. "What else do you fantasize about?"

Bloodied faces flashed before his eyes. Men he had killed. Men he had sent out on missions to be killed. Innocent women and children caught in the crossfire of war.

And with the images came the need that kept him alive.

But Abigail wanted fantasies, not a battle-scarred soldier's needs.

Before he could think of a lie, the cold, damp cloth trailed down his neck, his chest.

He groaned, knowing what was in store for him. And found that it was a fantasy of his. A fantasy that he had never known he possessed.

"You never answered my question earlier," she said, the cloth circling and circling a hardened nipple. "Is it as sensitive for a man here as it is for a woman?"

"Yes," he growled.

"Good." The cold cloth lifted. Only to be replaced by a scalding mouth.

He could feel the pull of her lips and tongue all the way down to his testicles. My god, he had never felt like this. Had never known that the male body was capable of this much sensation.

He grabbed the back of her head when she fed his nipple. "Don't stop."

"I'd read that a woman can orgasm from a man suckling her breast. Do you think a man can orgasm from a woman suckling his?"

Robert almost orgasmed at the mere thought. "I don't know."

He gritted his teeth, prepared for Abigail's next move. Only to find out that he was not prepared at all.

Schone proved what hundreds of romance writers had been longing to say: Women can handle a variety of erotic language and action; in fact, they love it. The irony is that the thinly veiled S/M tension that infuses every good romance novel has just barely been bridled all these years by the fear of a conservative or offended audience. The audience has always wanted more, but the publishers were the ones reluctant to tamper with a seemingly surefire formula.

I daresay that all successful romance writers are already masters of titillation, and I hope they have not been permanently disabled by pulling their erotic punches. The Wall of Coy has come down for good. You won't be able to write a romance novel tomorrow if you aren't prepared for sexual candor and female-centric points of view. Romance novels will be defined in the future by the drive and vitality of their female protagonists, rather than the salvation of their modesty and virtue.

- Think of three TV shows, either current or past, that you have a lot of memories and feeling for:
  Sci-Fi or Fantasy (*Star Trek, Xena, My Favorite Martian*)
  Crime Drama (*Law and Order, Colombo, Dragnet*)
  Situation Comedy (*Friends, The Brady Bunch, The Simpsons*)
- TV stories have very consistent characters and predictable plot lines. Take each one of your TV legends and write an explicit erotic scene that would fit into one of the episodes that you've seen a million times.
- Hate TV? Then take your genre/slash/fiction fun even further: Do the same exercise as above with traditional literature. Pick a fairy tale, a historical epic, and a religious myth. Now add a sex scene.
- Here's the extra bonus: Inevitably, the legends you choose will have sex included in their original version. Those old *Grimm's Fairy Tales* would make your hair stand on end if you saw the original texts, in uncensored versions like the recent edition translated by Jack Zipes. After you've finished your imaginary sex scene, go to the library or the Internet; look up Casanova in his unexpurgated glory. Compare your fiction with the sex and violence of the masters, and decide which one of you has outdone the other!

Which Genre Suits You?

Genre writing is something you do because you love it as a fan, and you are inspired by the masters of the style.

Favorite genres make such popular literature that many writers think they'll try their hand at a mystery, or a romance, for its commercial appeal. Don't make that mistake. You won't find any best-selling writers who found success by picking their genre like a stock. You have to have a passion for this. If you love genre writing, you probably resent that it's even called a "genre," because you appreciate its universal appeal and you've read enough of the work to respect its diversity.

Science fiction will always attract anyone who has a strong sense of the "What if?" as well as a background in legend and mythic tale-telling. Its best advocates are writers who understand the "old" as much as they seek to illustrate the outrageous, visionary, and contrarian.

Romance is the genre that has changed the most, because women's lives have changed the most since these stories first made the rounds in women's magazines. What romance writers will always be inspired by, however, is the dynamic heroine who defies the odds against her. She's a protagonist who never gives up on love.

In crime novels, we find the opposite of the romance charter— characters who resist the sunshine and flirt with self-destruction continuously, regardless of whether they're the good guys or the bad guys. Crime stories appeal to an author who wants to turn over the rocks, scratch off the veneer. Their idealism is only revealed in the sense that they believe that "the truth will out," regardless of who dies in the end.

Horror, like crime, takes the position that it's going to get ugly if you're ever going to get down to the bottom of something. Horror writers would rather reach into the dark, and drag in you with them, than sit poolside and only flirt with danger.

So—what if you wrote a book about a strong, unsentimental woman who nevertheless finds her most intimate desires satisfied, even though she has to slog thru murder, vengeance, and betrayal to get there? Plus, she has supernatural powers, and occasionally, she time travels.

Sounds like a pretty good novel to me, and I would wager there's already more than one author at work on something just like it right now. Genre writing is simply our modern-day fairy tales; they're the zest of the times, the icons we get thirsty for when we begin our own stories. You can drink from any one of them and find your own original niche. The first rule any genre master would tell you is: NO Rules. NO Genre. Break the mold while you caress it good-bye.

What Will People Say?

The biggest crisis for all erotic writers is wondering which feathers they're going to get tarred with when their sex work goes public. Will their intimate reveries be described as "purple" or as "pornographic"? Will their new title be the "Duke of Porno" or the "Queen of Smut"? Maybe you had something more dignified in mind.

In other cases, erotic authors may try their damnedest to be cutting-edge and raw, only to receive reviews that portray them as limp, pretentious, or effete.

No other genre outside erotica faces such a balancing act, where one strives to find such an elusive footing—where one's prose is neither too hard, too soft, too femme, too butch, too elite, nor too trashy. It's a Goldilocks drama where one never finds a spot or a taste that's "just right."

What makes erotic literature so difficult to appreciate? It's because the culture of American Puritanism—and its backlash, shame-based titillation—has set a scene in which any variety or imagination in erotic literature is always critiqued by the double standard. Are you naughty, or nice? Pervert, or saint? This is the kind of dogmatic judgment that awaits the erotic author's efforts.

Some of the geniuses of world literature have been called pornographers and smut peddlers. Some of the greatest and most dearly loved erotic stories were never embraced as art—or only after their originator was dead for fifty years. In order to survive as an erotic writer, you must take the Dadaist approach to critical responses. You must say to yourself, "A stroke book is an art book is a stroke book."

You are guaranteed to go crazy if you insist on defining "art" separate from "smut." No matter what conclusion you arrive at, you will never inspire, let alone enforce, a consensus regarding this canard. The Pope and the Supreme Court have already had their crack at it, without success, so why don't you give it a rest?

Your Worst Enemy

Here's the truth about "what people think"—the worst criticism, and the fiercest doubts you'll have about your own work, are going to rain down from one person: you. While it's true that a few writers have taken on the entire political and legal establishment to get themselves heard, 99.9 percent of the silencing that goes on in everyday self-expression is the result of your own self-policing.

Why do we shut ourselves up before anyone else gets an overt crack at us? Usually, we question our work by thinking of how a parent, spouse, or child might react. This is such a powerful prohibition. We're motivated to "shut up," partially out of love and protection, partially from fear and insecurity. That's an intoxicating mix, and it can silence just about anyone without further struggle.

The question of "coming out" with your erotic writing, or any kind of personal writing, is very much like the classic dilemma of the gay person in the family who wants to come out and wonders if s/he'll risk everything to do it. Will the family be shocked; will they act as if they don't know you anymore? Will they be ashamed; will they treat you like a criminal or a pervert? Will they blow up and then quickly get over it—or is it the beginning of the end? Will they simply look smug and say, "I always knew about you"?

Just contemplating their reactions is enough to make anyone

burn his or her diaries. Yet again, taking the cue from the gay coming-out model, it's rarely as bad as one imagines. The freedom you feel afterward is priceless. The "revelation" that you have sexual thoughts, and can express them, squashes the lie that you are a sexless creature altogether—and that's a good thing!

The courage you need is yours for the taking—just check out a few role models. Ask every erotic writer you can get your hands on if they're still close to their families. Most of them will tell you yes, and those who don't will explain that it's more complicated than the fact that they wrote a steamy scene in their last novel.

Ultimately, people with intimate connections don't just fall apart over these kinds of revelations. And here's another clue: The most stubborn family member, the one who rejects you the most harshly, is the one who is having the biggest battle controlling his or her own sexual feelings. So take a drop of sympathy before you condemn as well.

I don't live in some sex-positive bubble where rejection never happens. The first time I showed my mom one of my erotic publications, she sighed and asked me if I had thought about filling out an application at the post office. I gave her a copy of *Herotica*, which she later told me she never read. She never will! At the same time, she's told me she's so proud of me. She loves me to pieces, and even if she wishes I made my living at a nice civil service job, she and I are bound together in a way that can't be broken because of my sexual imagination! It's insulting to both of us to think otherwise.

I've also had lovers who were appalled at what I did. I was appalled that they were appalled! I would wonder how I could be hung up on someone who was such a prude. They would question how they could be so obsessed with such a bad girl. Ultimately, these relationships didn't work out, but respectful acceptance has taken the place of our once-fiery battles. We joke about it now, and at the end of the day, we'll joke about it a lot longer than we ever fought about it.

Some of you won't believe me. You'll think, "Susie Bright has no idea of what it means to be fried on a spit for uncovering your sexual thoughts." Whatever gory stories I could drag out of my scrapbook, I'm not sure what I could say to convince you of my experience, and empathy.

I do, however, have some practical advice for you: Write privately. Just because you write erotica doesn't mean that anyone else has to read it, or read it under your name.

Since you already know how to keep a secret, I don't have to give you tips on how to create a private place to write. Get your own postal box, a pseudonym, a safe with a lock—whatever it takes.

One of two things will happen. You will consciously, or unconsciously, reveal yourself. If you leave your diary open on the bathroom floor; if you tell everyone in town (except your spouse and kids) that you're giving an erotic reading at City Hall, don't act too shocked when you get busted. You were looking for an excuse; you found one. Now step up to the plate and start appreciating your new opportunities.

In the second case, you will guard your privacy successfully as long as you like. At some point, you may feel your work deserves a larger audience, and you will decide to change some of the terms of your privacy. But until then, you will have all the insights and pleasures of someone who has been writing her or his most intimate thoughts.

Get a Grip

Our society's dishonesty about sexual expression has resulted in a retarded erotic genre. Imagine a situation where we were condemned for publishing cookbooks that incited hunger, or mysteries that contained unbearable suspense. We would be a nation of people with no public taste and no thrilling curiosity. As it is, we're almost there: Our erotic taste and imaginations have been stifled and ridiculed beyond belief.

When an author embraces explicit sex along with other literary graces—comedy, tragedy, the sense of the times, the gender conundrum—we should be handing out awards, or at least gasping, "S/he told the truth!" How did these writers keep their natural feelings on the page? How did they manage not to self-censor, to corrupt and deny the muse? They thought with their dicks, with their clits—and what a discipline it turned out to be!

Yes, at a certain point, when you're finished writing, your attention will turn to seducing the critics and winning over an audience. But when you're composing your erotic story, you must, as a matter of necessity, push all the other voices out of your mind. You cannot write a book when you're thinking about selling a book; if you try, you'll have a writer's block the size of Madison Avenue. Stop thinking about perception and focus on conception. You need to retreat to your own world—to your privacy, your imagination—and write what pleases you.

Is Your Story Arousing?

Think about that word, *arouse*, on the most basic level. Your story may inspire readers to loosen their belt buckles on the spot, or it may linger in their thoughts as a nightly dream. It could make them cry, laugh, or scream in recognition. Your tale had better be "arousing" on some level, or you are going to have a terribly boring story on your hands. Your ability to arouse the emotions of your readers, and even their physical responses, is your gift, your hook. Don't ghettoize your story's erotic appeal, but think of it like any other strong emotion you might elicit from your reader.

Is Your Story Artful?

Artful, for a writer, means that you are graceful in your language, that you reveal a memorable voice, that you have timing and rhythm. Art is about drama and authenticity. Do you leave a mark? You'll be the first to know, because when you're writing well, you're the first reader to feel the excitement, that little bubble of euphoria.

Some writers get called "artists," and others get called "best-selling hacks." Some erotic writers get called "pornographers," while others are called "erotic visionaries." The bottom line is that if you have a gift to express yourself, and to communicate the human sexual condition, then you are both an artist and an acute observer of life. You need to savor and recognize when you're writing well, and to use those moments as your benchmark for creative reality.

Make a promise to yourself that while you are writing, you are not going to speculate about what color you're destined to be coded with. Whatever promises you made when you pitched the story, whatever expectations and clichés have been hitched to your star, you should dump them, pronto, when you pick up your pen. The critics, all the caricatures of sexual morals, they mean zero now, for they are not writing your story.

When the story is complete, in its first edited draft, then you can allow yourself to consider how you're going to spin it. You must be erotic now; you may be neurotic later, if you insist. Until then, keep your own counsel.

Don't ask yourself, "Is my writing stroke book material?" Instead, ask yourself, "Does my writing arouse the senses?" Instead of waiting for the director of MOMA to arrive and tell you that your work is "art," ask yourself, "Am I artful; am I giving my all?"

Part IV

Editing It

Editors: The Good, the Bad, and the Ugly

Writing and editing are the engines of any creative process that goes public. In their simplest form, writing and editing combine the genesis of an idea with its further consideration. We take our original expressions and hold them under the light of others' scrutiny. That scrutiny provides the moment of truth when you discover whether you are not only "expressing yourself," but also communicating with the rest of the world. Whether you simply decide to check your spelling, or rewrite your central thesis, the editorial process always makes the difference between mumbling to yourself and speaking to an audience.

There is one kind of writing that doesn't need an editor, and that's your private diary. But if you pass away and leave your private journal to posterity, then it, too, may be edited by your heirs and critics. In the end, the editor is there for you, waiting.

The challenge for all authors, once they've written their first drafts and wiped their brows, is to learn how to recognize and acquire good editors. The only thing worse than no editing is being edited at the hands of someone who is destructive, or an obstacle to your publishing ambitions.

Great Editors—and Good Ones, Too

In twenty years, I've had a handful of great editors, dozens of good ones, and a handful of screwups. The editors I've admired the most weren't the ones who caught every missing comma—they were the ones who could hear my voice and help me make it stronger. Every one of their suggestions, whether small or large, was considered in the style that best exemplified my signature. My favorite editors not only inspired my originality, they helped me put the razor's edge to it.

Great editors will have an outstanding command of the English language (facility in other languages doesn't hurt, either). But what makes them greater than other editors is their literary empathy— being able to channel your voice, knowing how you would say something. Superior editors have a background and a feel for your subject—they are worldly in the genre where you are competing. They love literature, they love news, they dote on words. They want your writing to reflect the best of you. They don't crave for your work to be more like their own—they thrive on the difference.

Great editors also get the big picture. They dream up new angles and topics that would be perfect for you, they're yentas for literary partnerships, they "imagine" you into new projects. Their instincts are superb. In total, they know how to exploit talent very, very well.

I've sometimes mistaken a great editor for something else. "Is s/he my best friend?" I've wondered, "or my ideal perfect shrink, or my dream lover?" Yes, sometimes an editor will be a friend, lover, or family member, but the ideal writer/editor relationship can and must exist entirely on its own. I've had some wonderful editors with whom I could hardly share a meal because we are such opposites in temperament. Our "match made in heaven" existed solely in our writerly dialogue, and I was happy to have it thrive in just that way.

Editors' sensitivity to your writing does not mean that they will know what to do about your love life, finances, or health problems.

If you make the mistake—as I have done!—of transferring nonwriting expectations to your editor, you shouldn't end the literary relationship when you discover your compatibility in other areas. A wonderful editor is someone you'll want to know until you die—it's a relationship to cultivate far beyond your current job descriptions and immediate futures.

What's a merely "good" editor? That's nothing to sniff at, either. Good editors will also be well educated and observant in your native tongue, and they'll have a reasonable familiarity with your subject and general style. You'll find that they make lots of great corrections and suggestions, but they will also make other comments that fall short, or don't quite match the way you would put things. It's then your job to politely restore your original language, or to suggest an alternative that suits your style.

If editors are good, they'll accept this interaction gracefully, and they'll pick up on what moves you. They recognize that there are plenty of ways to solve a problem of words or ideas, and they won't press you to accept their own alternative—unless it's the only option they believe will get your point across. They might not have your style down cold, but they will at least know how to come up with a neutral voice that doesn't compete with yours. In time, you might find your relationship has gone from good to great simply by practice and familiarity.

Bad Editor, Not Funny

Bad editors, by contrast, make for a lot of funny stories—in hindsight. They range from the truly unprepared—people who have been thrown a red pencil and crowned Editor for the Day—to seasoned editors who are so gnarled from jealousy, resentment, and petty slights that the only pleasure left for them is the spectacle of a writer on his or her knees. God help you if you encounter either one of these disasters—but I will offer some advice if you do, because the chances are rather likely.

The difference between the good editor and the evil one is often simply a matter of timing and compatibility. I've been an awful editor at times—because I was too green to know what I was doing, or I hated a story, or I was so vexed by the authors that I couldn't have decent rapport with them. I also, as an editor, have been blessed, praised, and honored. I have to bite my tongue before I diss another editor, because someone is probably telling an equally shocking story about me.

There's only one way to temper the inevitable roller coaster of new and uncertain editorial relationships. If you're publishing anything lengthy, noticeable, or important, then you need your own editorial counsel outside the publisher's office. Prepare this relationship in advance. That way, if you get your story back from a new editor who's clearly either a novice or a sadist, you have time to show it to your own mentor and get an objective voice. Is it you who's going crazy, or has the publisher's editor massacred your work? Having your own personal editor at hand will make all the difference.

In one of my books, the publisher's editor returned the manuscript to me with nearly every other word crossed out and replaced by a synonym. Every time I wrote something as straightforward as "She left," the editor changed it to "She departed." The substitutions were relentless, and my first impression was that I had somehow flunked basic writing.

I went to my personal editor, who had the advantage of not being soaked in tears and outrage, as I was. He took a five-minute look at the manuscript and said, "You have a writing style that uses a lot of Anglo-Saxon verbs, whereas your editor prefers to use Latin versions of all those same verbs. The Latinate style is more formal, like a legal document, but that's not what you're trying to convey here. Your own style is perfectly appropriate."

His quick analysis was a ray of sun parting my black cloud—I almost heard a heavenly chorus. As soon as he pointed out the editor's purpose, I could see it, too. I told my publisher in one sentence what the problem was, and she acquiesced to my decision. I could have flown further off the handle—but as a writer, preserving the integrity of my work was really the only goal I needed to pursue.

If you get a manuscript returned to you that seems strangely marked up—and you know that you were sober when you turned it in—you shouldn't hesitate to call your own editor(s) in. Don't even waste one day wondering whether you're a "bad writer" or whether you've "lost it"—you should spend that day showing your work to an outside referee. Your referee, of course, must be a pro—don't show it to a sycophantic fan just so you can have someone smooth your feathers.

You may be thinking, "But what if I *am* a novice writer, and what if I really *do* need a complete rehaul? What if I suck?" Maybe you're like my friend Cary, who has been known to submit work that went straight from his bong to the fax machine—he remains encouraged because his articles miraculously keep appearing in print, thanks to his enabling editor.

As an editor myself, if I receive work that is just badly written, or obviously sloppy, I don't waste one stroke of my red pencil on it. I call the author and ask what's up—or I reconsider the assignment. It would be insulting to both of us if I went through a paper with a continuous line of red ink. If the story needs rewriting, the author should have a chance to compose it again from scratch, before I take my turn.

I might even make the decision that I was wrong to employ this writer for this assignment in the first place, and kill the story. That may sound harsh, but it's a lot more compassionate than asking a writer to redo something he or she isn't prepared for, or didn't want to write in the first place.

That's one more element of a good editor: being willing to call the whole thing off, with grace and courtesy. Writers need to be matched well with their material and their audience. To ask a con-summate poet to perform as a dry technical writer is just cruel. When editors make a bad match, they need to be the ones to show some humility, not the author.

Bad editors, while not typically humble, usually know that they're blowing it—either because they're not experienced or because they've taken out their ego problems on their charges. They actually want to "look" good, and you might decide to help them do that if it's the best way to cut your losses.

I've had editors who wouldn't make it past a grade school gram-mar exam. But they're very grateful when I send back their pages, which I've had edited independently, with all the final corrections. My independent efforts cost me time, and maybe money, too; but if I want the work published, it's in my best interests to get the story edited professionally and move on. I can decide later whether I want to ever work with the inexperienced editor again.

Jealousy

Another mark of "bad" editors has nothing to do with their reading and writing talents. If you have any success at all in your publishing career, you may hear through the grapevine that certain editors claim that they "made" you, that you actually can't write at all, and that they had to doctor up everything you ever got into print. Your success is all due to them. The question will remain unanswered as to why, if they are so great, they haven't blossomed into wonderful writers themselves, without hanging so tightly to your coattails.

Whatever their motive, it doesn't matter—they have just violated the cardinal rule of Good Editorship: Thou Shalt Not Diss Thy Au-thor. Good editors take genuine pleasure in collaboration, but not at the expense of doubting a writer's originality. Great editors are se-cure in their work, and they know how to measure its weight. They don't have to pretend to be authors; they don't make themselves big at their authors' expense. Wonderful editors don't want to be you; they enjoy the esteem and confidence they've earned in their own right.

I have not always confronted editors who gossiped that I was a fraud—because, when their vanity is at stake, such people are not going to be in the mood to make amends. But I've certainly dropped all further publishing plans with them. Whatever I liked about our relationship, it was poisoned by such stories. The true confrontation happens as you move on to your next project. As soon as you publish something without a coattailing editor, it exposes the lie that the editor was the source of your success.

Finding the Perfect Editor

How does someone become an editor—good, bad, or otherwise? Every editor is a writer in some capacity, and all editors were once writers who realized they enjoyed critiquing and improving others' work. I think the first things I ever edited were high school term papers for my friends who were panicking before a big deadline. I enjoyed getting my two cents in; I liked seeing how other people wrote—editing was my voyeurism. I loved how grateful my friends were to me for helping them get an A. These simple sentiments I had when I was a novice are probably the basic emotions in every devoted editor's heart.

Later in my teens, when I worked as a newspaper journalist, I learned how short a deadline can be—and how quickly writing gets turned over into front-page news. There was no time for preciousness, and an absolute demand to write and edit like a pro. There's nothing that looks stupider than typos on a front page. A badly written story is a story no one reads, and no paper lasts long with that kind of track record.

The dailiness of editing is what makes someone good at it—doing it thousands and thousands of times. As a writer, you need to cultivate a certain level of editing expertise yourself. This, more than anything else, will help you identify editors you want to work with.

The first and most important editor in your writing career is yourself. Take the time to review and correct your own manuscript before anyone else sees it. You will win the reputation of being a good writer with clean copy. Those compliments should make your ears tingle and gain you tenure as a writer.

> **The Five Cardinal Rules for Editing Yourself**
> Work with the right tools.
> Take time between drafts.
> Read it out loud.
> Show it to a friend.
> Show it to a pro.

Working with the Right Tools

Paper, pencil, word processor, printer. A copy of *The Elements of Style*, a dictionary, a thesaurus, and a spell checker. The ingredients sound so simple, but ask any editor how many times he or she has opened an envelope only to find a "manuscript" that defies readability altogether. Who knows what it says? It's covered with goo, the printing goes faint on page 5, and the author's name doesn't appear anywhere on the page. The spelling rates a D-, and the author used the word *really* fifteen times in fifteen pages.

It's so hard to get published, why would any writer want to mess with the basic toolbox? If you think you can publish without using one of the items on my list, think again. If you think you can edit anything without these tools, you're kidding yourself.

Taking Time and Leaving Space—Between Drafts

Unless you are writing a formula report ("Man bites dog, film at eleven"), you cannot simply write a story, run the spell check, and then throw it at your editor for a magical rebirth. Stories of any kind, features of any kind, all need a chance to lie apart from you and be considered in a different frame of mind from when you first composed them.

I can't tell you where your brain goes when you're writing a story, but it's a little bit like a swooning crush. You have little objectivity, and your power of editorial analysis is disabled. It doesn't matter whether you're the kind of writer who agonizes between each sentence, or the one who dumps it all out in a half hour. Regardless of the time you took to write it, the five minutes after you've written "The End" is not the right time to review your piece. Your mind needs to move on to other things; you need to stretch your body, have a meal, a rest, an interaction that has nothing to do with your story.

The importance of quiet time and separation from one's first draft cannot be stressed enough. If you defy this advice and skimp on the time you need to consider your story before it leaves your hands, you will regret it. Your editor will send it back to you, and you will cringe at all the stupid mistakes you didn't catch. You'll realize that you missed a whole thought process you should have included. You didn't turn in a manuscript, you turned in Swiss cheese. It is to be hoped that you will conclude this humiliation by not repeating the conceit that you don't need to take a second glance at your genius.

As a rule of thumb, you never want to turn in a first draft—only a second, at the very least. If I have a story deadline for a Tuesday, and I want to cut it right down to the bone, I will write my story on Monday, sleep in it, and edit it Tuesday morning before I send it in. That's what I would call "cutting it close." My writing is best when I have at least twelve hours between readings. With a book-length work, I will look at it many more times than that, as do my editors.

Reading Aloud

You cannot self-edit by only reading silently. Your eyes move too quickly, your memory assumes too much. When you edit a story for the first time, you must read it aloud to yourself, and although you don't have to shout, you need to do more than move your lips. Read aloud as if you were reading to a friend. Every time you catch a typo, a clumsy phrase, or anything else you don't like, stop your reading and mark the paper with your pencil.

Don't try doing this "on screen" because you'll miss too much. It's not a natural position for reading aloud, which after all, is like a performance. You need to hold text in your hands.

Continue your reading, but don't belabor the parts you don't like. At this point, you need to hear the whole thesis aloud—if it's a book, one chapter at a time. When you're done, you'll have a well-organized list of the problems and errors you need to address in your next draft. Wash, rinse, do it again. Don't hand in your story to your editor until you are happy with a read-aloud version.

Share It with a Friend

I love sharing and reviewing my work with my closest friends and family members. Every page that goes out my door has been read by my partner, my father, and now, more frequently by my daughter, who thinks every story I write should include some homage to her. If I have friends visiting for the weekend, and a story is brewing on my computer, I can rarely resist showing it to them—or asking them to read it aloud so I can hear how it sounds in their voices.

My lover is a great listener because he has such keen political and psychological viewpoints; he always thinks of new angles and related stories for anything I come up with. He's like my own private *History of the World*, NPR, and CNN rolled into one.

My father is a remarkable editor himself—a linguist, a poet, and a writer. He has read more of everything than anyone I've ever met. Sending my stories to him is like sending them to Mount Olympus—he's the last word, as far as I'm concerned.

Finally, my daughter, I've realized, has a remarkable ear for dialogue—she can spot a phony line every time.

What do all these family members have in common? They love me, they are unconditionally supportive of my writing, and they get genuinely excited by what I'm doing.

Of course, I'm extraordinarily lucky to have such a devoted "in-house" editorial team. At the same time, I don't show my work to everyone I love or everyone I've befriended. Not all relationships cultivate that kind of give-and-take. If you're in the kind of family where everyone is at each other's throat, tearing each other down at each opportunity, then you're no more going to share your writing with them than you would with a bunch of sharks.

The difficult part comes when authors don't know whom to trust, when they make the mistake of sharing their hearts and manuscripts with someone who is carrying a hidden knife. Sometimes friends who were once your best ears can become jealous and resentful. It's even more sad when you lose an editor/friend to ill health, or to stresses that make it impossible to continue a familiar rapport. Losing a personal friend or family member who's been your writing and listening comrade is the worst—you'll feel abandoned, shocked, furious, helpless. If you write long enough, this will certainly happen to you at least once.

Nevertheless, editors who are part of your "tribe" offer affection, inspiration, and comfort that just aren't possible when you employ the considerable talents of professional editors. It's like the difference between great editing alone and great editing combined with great love. I will always take the risk of the latter, because that's really as good as it gets.

Share It with a Pro

You have the choice as an author to consult with your family and friends. But if your story is destined for the public, you will be edited by someone who is paid to review your work, whether you like it or not. You need to have your own professional editors to turn to.

If you get a manuscript back from your assigned editor, and you think the comments are dead wrong, you can't just go cry on your momma's shoulder—you need a pro's opinion at this point. You need a couple of editors you can turn to in a pinch. By paying them—or by trading on your friendship, goodwill, or great body—you must get them to survey the manuscript and the editorial work that's been done so far. Let them act as referees. For an article or short story, they'll need a few minutes to an hour to come to their conclusions. If it's a book, they'll need at least a few days to give you their initial impressions.

For book-length works, consider hiring your own editor. Unless you've worked with your publisher's editors before, or know their references well, you may be in for some big surprises. The editor who acquired your work may not be in the same position when it's time to edit your manuscript.

But if you hire a capable editor of your own choosing, you'll have, at the very least, a valuable second opinion, and in the worst case, you'll have someone working on your timetable, on your concerns, even if everything else falls apart. You won't feel like a schoolgirl waiting for your grade—you'll have already put your work under some scrutiny. Added bonus: Your publisher's editor will be happy that your manuscript is in such good shape.

Show your work to your agent, if you have one. Agents might not be editors, but they are surely readers. You need to get some feedback from people who are in the business of selling and marketing your work. Booksellers, publicists, and producers are also in this group. They need to know you, appreciate you, and give you some constructive criticism.

Your Very Own Focus Group

A writers' group—a gathering of two or more people who get together to talk about their ongoing work—provides a wonderful place to break the isolation of sitting alone in your room. You get to try out your stuff on supportive and educated peers. You might even find the editor of your dreams among the group's members. The sheer amount of laughter you'll enjoy from sharing horror stories is worth the whole pot of black coffee you'll consume.

Of course, we all know the parodies of the "bad" writing group— one that's dominated by a tedious narcissist, or another that's held in thrall by a politically correct bully. Finally, there are the cliques of Backstabbers Anonymous, or pseudotherapy groups that accomplish absolutely nothing. There's nothing to be gained by such bad chemistry except fodder for your future gossip columns.

But these are the exceptions. Good writers' groups are not so hard to find. If you're a student, teacher, freelancer, or on-staff writer, you already have the opportunities to make the kind of comradely friendships that lead to writers' groups. Find out who's offering writing workshops that you admire, and take one—seek out like-minded spirits.

In real writers' groups, you make your own rules, and you break them whenever you like. You can devote yourselves to critiquing stories in progress, to writing exercises, or to comparing contracts and editors. You can confide how your writing is affecting your family life, or other parts of your professional life. (Your family will be thrilled that it's not all dumped on them for a change!) You can compare dreams you've had the night before.

Keep your group small. A writers' group can be as few as two people; in fact, that's the description of one I'm in right now. The two of us meet once a week, and we each spend about an hour discussing the other's work. I feel so greedy for my friend's attention that I can hardly imagine sharing her with anyone else.

Too Much Editing

By now you may think, "Susie Bright has entirely too many editors." I've told you the benefits of family counsel, professional referees, and writers' group fellowship. Perhaps your image of writing was of a Waldenesque solitude—in which you'd craft perfect sentences and then fold them up in a bottle to set adrift on the sea. I hope that you at least read your soliloquy aloud, and run a spell check, before the tide washes it all away.

My combined chats with various friends and editors about my work occupy perhaps one to four hours a week, total. They involve an E-mail message here, a dinner conversation there, my weekly writers' meeting, or a phone call at my desk. Yet my writing time—when my door is shut to everyone, and my typing fingers alternate between sweat and chill—is thirty to fifty hours a week. I have solitude in spades.

I also have a stubbornness in my work, and I'm not all that patient. If I was showing my work to someone who made remarks like "You spelled 'kaleidoscope' wrong again," I wouldn't come back for advice a second time. Neither could I stand someone who just patted me on the head and gave me a gold star. Good editorial feedback is, at its essence, a wonderful conversation. It's not tedious or insulting, or a bunch of feel-good drivel.

Do you deserve good editors and counsel you can trust? Absolutely. If you're working as hard as you should be, if you're writing virtually every day, then you need editorial criticism and the editorial inspiration. Anything else is an amateur deception.

The Editor Search: A Few Dos and Don'ts

- Get references from other writers about editors they've worked with and enjoyed.
- Don't send your work *unsolicited* to authors you admire. Treat them like professionals: Ask them if they take on individual mentoring or editing projects, and inquire about their fees.
- Look on the Internet for book doctors and freelance editors. Many consulting editors have put up Web sites where they explain their work in detail, show examples, and give specific references. This is one great way to get acquainted with the kind of work they do.
- Don't "squeeze" other writers. If you are a friend of an author—not a long-lost pal from a decade ago, or a one-night stand, but close friends—then by all means approach. But have realistic expectations; authors write every day for a living.
- If you want to cold-call a few professional editors to inquire about their private editing services, then go for it, with compliments and checkbook in hand. You would be wise to choose an editor with considerable experience in magazine and/or newspaper editing. There are fantastic book editors and academic editors, but if you're pulling names out of a hat, the bar of printed periodical editorship is where you'll find the largest quantity of focused and prolific experience.

Copyediting and Proofreading

A **poorly edited** book is a big cringe. My stepmother says putting out a manuscript without adequate proofing is like giving someone a big smile without realizing that you have spinach on your teeth.

The humiliation caused by errors in your text will make the whole body of work lose credibility. Among friends, of course, who's to complain about a misspelled word or a dropped apostrophe? But between reader and author, such things make the author look illiterate and careless. It's unfair, it's brutal—but in the end, you must submit! You'll sleep and write better with a beautiful clean manuscript on your desk.

Editing is what happens when you are still working with major issues, both in the content and in the structure of your piece. This is not the time when it's crucial to catch every misplaced comma, but you can certainly change anything and everything in this phase.

Copyediting corrects spelling, grammar, usage, and punctuation; it ensures that the manuscript is consistent and accurate, checks cross-references, and prepares the style specifications for publication.

Proofreading, the most fine-grained of all the editing phases, happens when the manuscript is in good enough shape so that it doesn't need any further copyediting. Proofreaders check the text for mechanical errors—including typos, problems with typesetting specifications, and page makeup. In proofreading, you compare the latest stage of the project to earlier stages, and you make sure that changes have been entered correctly.

It's really quite daunting to realize how much labor and meticulous detail go into a well-prepared book. It always takes more than one pair of eyes, because authors can never see all their own errors. Furthermore, proofreaders have a special type of eye; it's well worth your time and money to hire or seduce a good one.

One night I was reading a *New York Times Magazine* collection of stories by New Yorkers describing their first year in living in the city. Liz Smith, the well-known entertainment reporter, recalled her first job at *Newsweek* in 1949, working as a proofreader. In those days, reporters worked in teams that were called the "pitcher" and the "catcher"—one person read aloud every single word and punctuation mark that appeared in a story, and the other would put a pencil dot over each word in the manuscript to indicate it was satisfactory.

Computers, with their spell checks (good) and grammar checks (bad!), have given the publishing world the impression of things' moving faster, with less human error. But as you can see from the varying state of clean copy in your daily newspaper, there is no substitute for a real person editing in real time. If reading aloud was the gold standard for *Newsweek* in American publishing's golden years, it's a good example for you today. Open wide, and don't cop out.

In the final result, a well-edited book is worth all the trouble. The reader will never even notice all that sweat and fuss—the book will simply look as if it appeared whole and perfect in its first incarnation.

In this book, while I've been busy lecturing and scolding on the essentials of good editing, my greatest fear has been that my own readers will find errors in my own text. If you do find such errors, you will have the proof before your own eyes that such mistakes can be embarrassingly common, and yet distracting. If you are gracious, you will notify me immediately so I can correct the next edition!

Part V

Publishing It

A Devil's Argument Against Publishing

f you write an erotic story—or any story, for that matter—and never publish it, you will have done a very good thing. If it stays in a box for you to cherish, if it is passed between you and your lover, shared among friends, or circulated on a private E-mail list, you will have accomplished something quite wonderful.

By writing privately, you will have expressed yourself intimately and communicated with exactly whom you wanted to speak to in the first place. You will have the primal satisfaction of an artist: your imagination fulfilled. You'll have confronted the challenge to be authentic, to dream aloud, to take yourself over the falls and climb back out, soaking wet and ready for the next round. Congratulations, you are a true writing hero!

By *not* publishing in the public world—with the mediation of publishers, distributors, and retailers—you will remain unsullied and unembittered by the publishing process, which is not unlike being dragged naked inside a barrel filled with nails. No one will put a price on you, no series of twits will be the final arbiters of your value. Your writing will not be lost in the shuffle, or ignored, or insulted. It won't find itself in the hands of the indifferent and indignant. You won't be told you're a superstar, but neither will you ever be called a has-been, a one-shot wonder, or a fraud. You will not be betrayed by strangers.

When I read stories by unpublished writers that deeply affect me, I am torn. My first impulse is, "They are so incredible, they must be read by the rest of the world. How can I get their work in print?" Yet the other side of me says, "They are so dignified in their publishing innocence, their uncompromised integrity. How can I seduce them into what I know is a miniature version of hell?"

My advice to unpublished writers is this: There is nothing like the thrill of reaching new readers with your work, the people who resonate with your creative ideas and want to share their own inspirations with you. There is nothing like hearing a total stranger say, "Your story changed my life." Some of those strangers will become your dear new friends, future collaborators, lovers, and comrades.

However, in order to reach those new friends, lovers, and comrades, you are going to have to go to The Market. The Market is not "your friend"; The Market does not have your self-interest at heart. It can be an intoxicating place—the money changing hands, the competitions, the auctions, the promotions and premiums—but it isn't a place that puts art first, or people first. It puts money first, and that requires a measure of illusion and exploitation that must be endured in order to reach your desired audience.

The fans of The Market will snarl at you, "If you can't take the heat, get out of the kitchen," and it is best to take their words as helpful advice rather than as an insult. There is no dishonor in being an artist who simply doesn't want to get burned. If you do go The Market route, you will, without exception, get burned, and so you have to be the sort of person who tolerates scarring.

I have looked over my publishing career many times, trying to weigh its consequences. I've met thousands of wonderful readers and fellow writers. I've been influential; my I'm-going-to-change-the-world tendencies have been powerfully stoked. I've supported my family with my writing, and I've also indulged in luxuries, the most delicious of which has simply been the fortune to not work a nine-to-five job. It's been an ego trip par excellence; it's been a cash cow; it's been a dream come true; it's been a revolution in my life as an artist and, in my case, as a social activist. Those are the benefits

The Market allowed me, although it has never, ever given me the insight and pleasure I get from sitting down at my computer to write. That high is mine alone.

The Market has also been a beast to me, in the same way that it is to all writers, whether famous, rich, or practically anonymous. I've submitted to people I don't respect. I've agreed to compromises that made me sick and kept me awake nights. My work has been placed in the hands of people who were incompetent, frightened, and even malicious. I've lived on a financial roller coaster, with my heart in my mouth, and caused my family no end of worry. Bad reviews and unsparing personal criticisms have been de rigueur, and so have stalkers and sycophants. And my case is hardly unique. I'm only traveling down a road as weathered as a Roman highway.

The more well known and successful you become, the more you are a target of others' envy and your own insecurity. Someday you will wake up understanding perfectly what *they* want, but not having a clue what *you* want anymore. Your own personal insights may feel bleached and dovetailed into the desires of those you aim to please. Sometimes you will hate writing, and think you'd rather be boiled in oil than suffer another deadline, another contract, another publicity stunt. You will verge on complete misanthropy. Some of the indignities—the greatest ones—will be hidden from you and remain that way for years.

The professional writers' philosophy, like the motto in academia, is "Publish or Perish." Those of us who've survived years in publishing are masochistically proud, like war veterans, of our head wounds, our shaking hands, and our lack of a bath. For us, to have made contact with a new audience—to have made *contact*, period—was worth the struggle in The Market's trenches. We like to tell the story about how we nearly died—a hundred times over.

But as much as I'd like to offer another toast about how I triumphed over The Market, how I made it dance my tune, I'd rather be candid for a moment: I admire writers who don't publish or who self-publish. It's not their craft or their content I speak of, but rather their dignity, their discretion, their complete control of their work.

For those little piggies who don't go to The Market, who stay home, who write what they want and swallow none of the garbage, I salute you, and I encourage you to stay the course. Your creative spirit is second to none, and as regards your erotic understanding and satisfaction, you will only benefit from the pleasures of never being deemed a commodity. Relish it!

Money Money Money

One of the most popular reasons to write—and to write about sex in particular—is to make money. Our national advertising motto always has been Sex Sells, and most people believe that anything that titillates the libido will score big in the marketplace.

The financial reality of selling sex writing is very different from the hype. Yes, there is an income to be made at erotic writing, but most of those incomes are fit for a mouse—few are fit for kings.

By far the easiest way to sell erotica is to be content with a small payment—something that makes you feel like a professional but nothing that you would depend on for your monthly nut. In this scenario, you would tell people without blinking that you are a writer, you would be able to show your published work, and you would have the satisfaction of purchasing nice meals and sentimental gifts with your royalties. You could even become quite famous and well respected in your genre, with a great deal more attention paid to you than money. You could even go down in history, but it won't be because of your bank account.

There are three kinds of working writers: those who write for an auxiliary income, those who write full-time, and those who write for mammoth fortune and fame.

If You Want to Make *Some* Money at Writing—
but Not a Full-time Livelihood

Output: You need to write and complete work often enough
   that you don't completely drop out of sight—once or twice
   a year at a minimum.

Talent: You need to have at least an occasional burst of talent—
   at least one good idea that you will be remembered for.

Skill: You need friends or mentors to help get your professional
   act together. When you offer your work for sale, someone
   has to make it look good, in its presentation, in addition to
   its inherent quality.

Ambition: You need enough ambition and ego investment in
   your work to make some phone calls—or else show up in
   person to ensure that your writing sees the light of day in a
   fashion that you can be proud of. You need to have some
   people skills, or get someone else competent to front for you.

Luck: You need luck, and you will inevitably have some. But
   when you do, you can't kick it in the face—or turn your
   heel and think it will get even better tomorrow. You need to
   cultivate at least one good relationship in the publishing
   market to help you get your work out, and if that one ex-
   pires, you will need to replace it, or else you'll suffer the
   same demise yourself.

Prudence: You don't have to be prudent financially at this stage,
   because you're not relying on a writer's income to sustain
   yourself.

Advocates: You don't need an agent, manager, tax accountant,
   or entertainment lawyer. You're not investing your time in
   protecting your business interests, you're solely interested
   in your creative investment. You can benefit by having loved
   ones who support you, who love to see you writing, and
   who give you their honest appraisals of your work.

If You Want to Make a Living at Writing—
Year In and Year Out

Output: You must be extremely prolific. You must write and brainstorm on schedule, with deadlines and goals, virtually every day of the week.

Talent: You must have a gift and talent that consistently deliver to your fans what they love best. You must have oodles of ideas and a very active imagination.

Skill: You must master the professional tools and rules of the trade: reliable writing equipment, sound editing and proofreading skills, the formats and courtesies of editorial correspondence.

Ambition: You must be ambitious; you must be driven to get people's attention at every level of the publishing chain: editing, marketing, sales, and publicity. You must not only write, you need to enjoy talking about your work and thinking up ideas to promote it. You must meet your readers, your booksellers, the media, and the people involved in the production process. You must consider the marketing of your book to be just as essential as writing it in the first place. You can't risk deep depressions or slumps because of criticism or rejection. More than anything, your ambition must be consistent and not easily fatigued.

Luck: You need good luck and fortuitous timing. But, more important, you need the know-how and the disposition to take advantage of fortune every time it winks at you. Everyone will get some luck, some time—but some people will blow it, and others will walk on by as if it could be encountered any day of the week. Successful writers find it almost impossible to ignore a lucky situation. They can't resist taking up a lead, even if it means ignoring other pressing business. They are invigorated by risk, and consider blind faith in their talent to be an asset.

Prudence: Over time, commercially successful writers seek to cushion themselves from the inevitable volatility of the publishing market. You will have great stories that still won't sell; you will encounter production and distribution setbacks. Your work will be preempted by everything from natural disasters to political scandals.

In order not to go down in flames every time you hit a bump, you have to find a way to support your writing career in bad times as well as good. That means avoiding debt; it means consistent investments and careful insurance; it means diversifying your writing talent.

Critics may call you a "national treasure," but they don't give you a line of credit when your coffer is empty. You have to be open to the idea of teaching, performing, consulting, editing, advertising, and working outside your favorite genre. You'll need to safeguard your health, and you must treat your physical ability to write as if it were a pair of million-dollar legs insured by Lloyds of London.

Advocates: You need a Big Dog; in fact, you need a pack of Big Dogs. If you are writing as much as you need to be, you need an agent to sell your work and defend your business interests. You need someone to navigate the tax system for you. You need legal help from your agent or attorney to protect your copyrights and enforce your contracts. You need relationships with other writers to promote and define your group interests.

You might find that you enjoy doing some of these advocacy activities yourself, but they are full-time professions, so at some point you will have to make up your mind: Do you want to be a writer, or a writer's advocate? Whether you like advocates or hate them, you will be eaten alive by the publishing market if you do not enlist their help.

Finally, you need personal advocates—people who simply love you, no matter what, and believe in you at every turn. "Ain't we got love!" might be the only music playing in your career some days, and you'll be grateful for it.

How to Write a #1 Bestseller—and Never Write Again If You Don't Want To

Output: You need one killer idea, and it has to be something you're willing to live with as your legacy for the rest of your life.

Talent: You don't need to know how to "write"—at all. Only your one excellent idea is required. However, you do have to recognize good writing, because if you don't write your story, then you will be hiring someone, a ghostwriter, to do this part for you. This person will need to have excellent writing skills, and you will need good chemistry with him or her so that your ideas can flourish in his or her hands.

As for your erotic ideas—you're unlikely to be #1 with a book that is purely sexual. But if you take your erotic ideas and integrate them into an already popular genre like romance, mystery, history, or self-help, then you might have a potential bestseller on your hands.

Skill: Again, craft is not required in this case—you'll be contracting those duties out. But you will need excellent people skills—a genuine talent and charisma at getting people to notice you. You need to look good, and especially to look good on TV. In fact, it's much more important for you to look good in pictures than in real life. Your appearance, your style, your speaking voice will all play a starring role in your book's promotion. Even if you thought you got off easy by not having to write the damn thing, you will work your ass off promoting it for years to come.

Ambition: Unsinkable is the key word here. You need to think beyond ambition—you must have destiny in mind, a sincere dose of narcissism, and an unstoppable need to prove something. People will say this is your fatal flaw, and, sadly, it may well be, but you won't reach "overnight success" without it.

Luck: You need that one-in-a-million chance. Happily, you're the kind of person who believes in perfect connections; you already think you're lucky and deserve the best of fortune. You're impatient to make it happen—you're counting the minutes. With this in your character, you will not be whiling away the hours in a small town, working on your embroidery. You move to the hot spots, you position yourself in the thick of it, you go out at night, and you schmooze all day. You identify people with power in an instant, and you're masterful at cultivating their acquaintance. You are a charming son (or daughter) of a bitch.

Prudence: When it comes to money, you want it big, you want it all up front, and you treat it like capital, not pocket change. The lion's share of your money goes into furthering your career and into diversified, sound investments. Your attitude is not "I'm an artist," but rather "I'm a rising corporation." You take your great book idea and turn it into a million other products and services.

If you're the sort of person who realizes you'd rather blow it all on hookers, cocaine, and caviar, then you buy yourself a gorgeous diamond leash and hand it to the most conservative person you know—then tell that guardian to put it around your pretty little neck and hold on tight.

Advocates: In your kind of success, you don't need a Big Dog, you need a Saber-Toothed Tiger. Your business interests need round-the-clock protection and relentlessly aggressive advocacy. You find out who the best people are employing, and you employ them as well. You build a stone firewall around yourself, and you don't go crying to the *National Enquirer* about how lonely it is at the top. You've built your gilded cage, and you'd better learn how to sing a song you enjoy.

Your greatest challenge will be to retain a few friends who knew you before you were rich and famous and who don't need your money or notoriety to stay your pals. These are not advocates that you could employ, although many people might want to be your friends for a fee.

In this situation, your loyalty will become paramount in ways that are irrelevant to the publishing market. The Market doesn't reward faithfulness—whether it's New York or Hollywood—but true friendship and love need unswerving loyalty to survive. If you don't have any friends or family who'll stick by you when you're "king of the world," then you will, without a doubt, regret that you ever achieved this position. Think of your true friends often, and early, on your climb to the top.

My First Breaks

I started out as a writer who never dreamed of being paid to be published; I was just thrilled to see my work on paper. I had absolutely no career plans in writing. I didn't take writing classes; I didn't pursue my craft. I wrote whenever I was feeling passionate—when I was in love, or moved to tears by something I read in the newspaper. I was a prolific letter writer; I liked to record my dreams and keep diaries. But I made my money waitressing, cleaning, and working in factories, on farms, at switchboards, and in retail operations. I rarely made over minimum wage, and I never stayed anywhere more than six months. I had no one to support except myself, and all my belongings fit into one army trunk.

When I was twenty-seven, after fifteen years of publishing in little-known or underground publications, I got an offer to write one column for *Penthouse* magazine, paying $1,200 a month. It was my first regular-paying gig, and the first time anyone had offered me significant money. The editor had been reading my work in my counter-cultural sex magazine, *On Our Backs*, and he thought I was funny and quick.

The money *Penthouse* offered seemed like a fortune at the time. I couldn't quit my day job fast enough. I went out and had oysters, I bought some really great shoes, and I rented a little writing studio space so I'd have somewhere quiet besides the kitchen table to write.

Over the next few years, I began to publish my first books. I had no help in negotiating my contracts. I didn't understand most of the contract language, but I was very eager. I was thrilled if my publisher gave me a month's rent to begin the process.

Within five years, I was very proud of all my freelance and book work—I enjoyed writing and editing more than ever. But I realized, financially, I had screwed myself with both my ignorance and my lack of an advocate. As someone brought up with working-class values about money, I had a lot to learn about concepts like "savings," "investments," and "insurance." I didn't have a clue about how to be an entrepreneur. I didn't have a union steward who was going to negotiate my contracts, and no one was going to go on strike if I got a bad deal.

In 1990, I got into my first legal battle over intellectual property rights, and I needed a lawyer. By that time, I saw that I'd destroyed any hope of decent royalties from the past contracts I had signed, and I was afraid to sign another until I got on better footing. I needed an agent, and I went looking for one, the same way some women look to get married. I was desperate, and I was determined.

Right at that juncture, I got my first offer from a major New York publisher. In a rare—and I realize now—almost-unheard-of gesture, the editor lowered his voice a bit and said, "Susie, you would do yourself a great disservice to negotiate this contract without an agent. If you don't know anyone good, I can give you some names."

That is the first and only time that a representative of a publishing company has ever recommended something that was entirely in my interest. I got an agent and negotiated the first five-figure advance I'd ever received.

Up to this point, what I'd had on my side was talent, a strong work ethic, ambition, and a gregarious personality. It was hard for me to realize that I was lucky, because I had been involved in loser causes for so long that I always thought I'd be the underdog. I had been a socialist in the Reagan years; I was out of the closet before most people knew where the door was; I was a folk music enthusiast when everyone else was into disco. When I started *On Our Backs* with my friends, and we hatched our plans to do a radical women's sex magazine, the last thing on my mind was "Won't we be rolling in dough!"

When *On Our Backs* debuted in 1984, the world of sexuality, gender roles, and desktop publishing was about to explode. Quite by accident, I was at the front of the line. I always thought women should be outspoken about their sexual desires—but in the late 1980s, I found myself lifted onto the shoulders of thousands who felt the same way, and I was subsequently telephoned by businesspeople who saw dollar signs when they checked out an erotic revolution.

My *Best American Erotica* deal in 1993 gave me my first taste of professional advocacy, and my introduction to prudent money management. What's more, my work was going high profile; I was being invited to write for the most popular magazines and newspapers in America. I was lecturing at universities all over the country; I was on TV and radio. For once, those new shoes came in handy—I looked really good. My sexual confidence and my writing chops were red hot. It seemed like everyone wanted to talk to a "do-me feminist," a "feminist pornographer," the "goddess of women's erotica."

I found a great agent and we negotiated my first six-figure deal. I found myself the object of desire at a hysterical book auction, with the top publishers vying over who would get me to be their new, hot, sex girl. The kind of thing they thought was "hot," I considered about ten years out of date—but who was I to argue with their bountiful enthusiasm!

But I still had a lot to learn about "bounty." A $100,000 deal became $80,000 after I paid my managers, and $60,000 after taxes. The advance was paid over the course of two years, so I would get $30,000 to live on for the first year, and the balance when I turned in the manuscript and they accepted it. With a California mortgage to pay, and a family to raise, writing a book full-time for $30,000 was hopeless. So I worked at freelancing and lecturing all year long to make up the rest. My editor left the publisher after the deal was struck; then my next editor left when my book was about to come out. My original publisher had been bought by another publisher.

At the time, these episodes horrified me; I thought my "luck" was up. I had never imagined that events beyond my control would be the deciding factor in whether the world heard about my new book. This was before I realized that such events in The Market are to be expected. If you keep the same editor at a big publishing house from the time you sign the contract to the time the book hits the stores, you have witnessed a miracle as profound as Mary's immaculate conception. If your big chance to go on TV, to talk with someone intelligent about your book, isn't canceled due to a killer tornado, or an

O.J.-style car chase taking over your time slot, then you just haven't been paying attention. If your publisher doesn't have a stock disaster or isn't an object of a hostile takeover, then you must be on Mars, not in New York.

Still, my big-time book deal was better than a kick in the pants. It raised my profile and my asking price as an author. I bought a home; I raised my daughter. I invested in my business, paid off my credit card debt, started a retirement account.

When I was first writing in San Francisco, I was fortunate to become friends and colleagues with many other talented people, some of whom found themselves on a trajectory like mine, climbing up the publishing ladder. A few of them secured huge deals, seven-figure advances on their royalties; and although sometimes my first reaction was envy, I realized over time that they faced the same issues of prudence and advocacy down the road as I had. Their writing ability and enthusiasm were challenged seriously by the demands of The Market, just like anyone else.

Another caveat: Any writer over twenty-five will experience serious health issues in a professional writing career. I had thought I was getting out of blue-collar health hassles when I became a professional writer, but that was before I got pneumonia two years running, each time I did a book tour. Book writing might only give you carpal tunnel syndrome and a fat ass, but book promotion can just about kill you—it requires sleep deprivation, inadequate nutrition, and daunting amounts of drugs just to perform the basics. I'm not just talking about the intoxicants, but rather all the antibiotics, steroids, anti-inflammatories, sleeping aids, and wake-up goosers. Touring, like any MTV legend will tell you, is not natural for the human body.

Even the most successful writers also experience failure: a book that doesn't sell, a kamikaze critic, a publisher that runs off with the till. It's show business, not just a book business, and you're only as good as your last curtain call. Writers are called upon to reinvent themselves more times than Madonna ever dreamed of—and it's something we're often attracted to, because of our overactive imaginations.

I like making my livelihood as a writer. I once said that I didn't want to do anything else, and lately it's occurred to me that I *can't* do anything else. I enjoy promotion and the business side of my work; I like thinking about how I'm going to pull my next rabbit out of a hat.

Yet the system for publishing books, as it stands, is hardly my utopia. Writers and their artistic talent should be nurtured and cherished. Our stories are the heart of human connection; we are the deliverers of history and myth. We are Pandora and everything that's in her box, including the hope.

Big-time publishing means big-time money—a great big print
run, a great big name on the cover of your book, and a great big
hullabaloo over you. The big-time excitement might expire within
hours or run breathlessly for years.

There are many misunderstandings about big-time publishing,
more than other kinds of presses, and perhaps that's because corporate book publishing is such an oxymoron. Media moguls from
the movie and recording industries, who have acquired all the big
book companies in recent years, look at the accounting books in
their book-publishing offices with undisguised horror. They can't believe all this work has gone into such a low profit margin.

Unlike the mass media, where nothing is released unless it appeals to the lowest common denominator, books have been published
throughout history for millions of small and unique audiences. There
are books about hedgehogs, and about inflatable blow-up dolls—
each genre has its small band of devotees. When readers go to bookstores, they expect to find a world of choices open to them. No one
wants to walk into a favorite bookshop only to find that the number
of titles has been reduced to ten or twenty "favorites" that "everyone"
is supposed to enjoy. The book business won't run that way.

Variety and diversity are keys to book lovers' happiness, but
they're no thrill for businessmen looking for a big bang. Book companies have always been run by businessmen, but they used to be the
sort of gentlemen who, for one reason or another, could tolerate the

low margins made by bookselling—and who wanted, for themselves, the esteem awarded for a great legacy.

That era is over. The common sentiment now among book publishers is that, if something doesn't sell over 100,000 copies, it's hardly worth cutting down the trees and providing the paper to print it. New and veteran writers are under incredible pressure to either put up big numbers, through sales or subsidiary deals (like film rights), or get out of the game. This is quite startling when you consider that some of the most influential books in history never came close to selling that number, and never got made into a movie. Look at the References pages in the back of this book—these are all books that have shaped our erotic culture as we know it—but the majority of them have never sold anywhere near six figures.

I've had several national bestsellers, and I certainly take pride in that accomplishment. But a "national bestseller," in the trade, means that you are in the top-ten list of at least two major markets—say, Boston and Chicago, or San Francisco and Denver. That's all well and good, but in terms of numbers, such a distinction does not necessarily mean you've broken into six-figure sales.

I once had the pleasure of being on the *L.A. Times* bestseller list right after the Harry Potter books, which took the first three spots. I was delirious with excitement. I called my publisher to ask her if she would consider advertising my book, at least regionally, now that I had hit such a prominent local position.

"I hate to disappoint you, Susie," she said, "but the only books on that list that are selling in any great numbers are Harry Potter—you and everyone else in the last seven places are just treading water."

The financial success of a book will only be noted when it is a *New York Times* bestseller. That is the only distinction that means anything in terms of commercial worth. Anything less, by a large publisher's pocketbook, is debatable.

This somewhat depressing background is necessary to know for any author who's seeking a big-time publishing deal, because your watchword in such an endeavor must be: It's Not Personal—and It's Not About Literature.

The great fear that novice erotic authors have about approaching large publishers is that the editors will be embarrassed by explicit subject matter, that sex writing is too radical for them—that they will blush and "not understand."

This is not true at all. Most men who run these book companies have not been embarrassed since someone pantsed them in the third grade, and they are hardly gong to be blushing around you. They don't care how radical you are; they don't care what your message is. They don't care if your first sentence is about doing it doggie-style with your dad on the Heathrow runway—they only want to know that it can sell. This is a Big-time Crap Shoot, and they want to know if you look lucky. You are a pair of dice that is going to be thrown on the green, and if you don't hit it right the first time, the game will move on.

To pitch a book idea to the big publishers, you have to understand the nature of the bestseller list, develop a feeling for the pop culture zeitgeist, and have your arguments ready for why your idea has a chance to be in the top ten.

First, the sexual character of your novel must be in the context of a popular genre: memoir, historical, romance, mystery, diet book, etc. If your book idea is "I want to tell people how really important sex is and why they should spend more time thinking about it in their lives," you're going to get absolutely nowhere. It's not because your thesis is wrong, or because anyone is offended. Rather, it's because the last time anyone saw a book like that in the top ten it was Alex Comfort's *The Joy of Sex*—a book that couldn't get a bus ticket out of town today.

The sexual revolution as a "news item" is not relevant today on the mass scale that it was in the 1970s. Yes, there's interest in Viagra, pornography, "vaginal rejuvenation," etc., but it's nothing, sales-wise, like the tidal wave of gender and sexual transformation that was ushered in by the 1960s counterculture. Sexual liberation has been mainstreamed, which is great, but it's no longer the "Next Big Thing."

Publishers don't blanch at controversial topics if they're in a context they believe is salable. Incest, queer longings, cannibalism? Bring it on, if that's your fancy. What the publisher wants to know is how you plan to compete. Your idea is worthless without a marketing plan and a survey of the competition.

Big-time publishers like big-time names—because they know how much name recognition means in sales. But they also like the newcomer, the ingenue, the first-time author they might be able to make into a star. They will often give you a couple of chances to get your sales numbers up if they think you look like you've got "legs."

What they don't get excited about are authors in the middle: writers who've been selling books for years but don't have a name—or who have a name but whose sales didn't break through the roof their last time out. Like gamblers, publishers like fresh fillies and sure things, and they're suspicious of runners they believe are past their peak.

Of course, many midlist authors scream, "What do you mean, 'my peak'? The only reason my last book didn't hit the top is because your marketing department crumbled to its knees!"

But publishers aren't big on what they didn't do. It's all about the photo finish for them. If you didn't win, no matter whose fault it was, they don't want to see a loser.

Nevertheless, if you get a serious big-book deal, you should go for it, and suit up for the ride. They are going to pay you an advance that will allow you to write without interruption—the ultimate writer's luxury—and they will also work on your behalf for the book's promotion. Their distribution network is unparalleled, and you would never be able to compete with it as a self-publisher, or through an alternative press.

The big-book publisher will probably not be as enthusiastic, or devoted, or creative as you would like, but even so, their efforts will save you considerable time, postage, and phone bills. They are assuming some of what would otherwise be your overhead. They are opening up your book to a world that would otherwise never see it. Picture that shopping mall bookstore in Indianapolis, and Houston, and Duluth, and Spokane. Your book is there.

The Changing of the Guard

There are some things that big-time publishers *used* to do but that they no longer specialize in. Authors can't afford to waste any sentimental tears about the changing of the guard.

Prepare yourself: You are not likely to have an experienced print editor. That is, it's unlikely that your editor will have the training, experience, and talent that are traditionally associated with the editing profession. Editors will not be able to help you on the deep levels of your craft, or even more superficially. They are not likely to be intellectuals, or great readers, or have any particular interest in your subject.

You need to ask for the references of every editor assigned to you. Ask them for copies of books they edited, and the contact info for those authors. Then read the books and call the authors. They'll tell you what their editorial experience was like—they're probably dying for someone to ask.

You might get lucky, and be impressed with your editor's references. Ask for a home phone number, because you'll probably want to know this editor forever!

But then there's the not-so-lucky—a predicament you should be ready for.

When I was young, visiting one of my first big-time publishers, I met my new editor there, and I was eager to make a sympathetic connection. I asked him what his background was. "Not much really," he said. "I was a tie salesman until a few months ago."

Until proven otherwise, you must assume that your editor is a former tie salesman. Most book editors today are not experienced line editors, but beyond that, they also do not have any power to make deals with you. The real deal makers are the sales managers, who have power over whether your book flies or not. They, in turn, are under the pressure of buyers at chain bookstores. The chain buyers and the sales managers do not speak to authors, and only rarely to agents. They might not read your book at all, but it's their decision to sell it or not.

Given that your editor might be a metaphorical tie salesman, what do you need to do? First, you must acquire an actual, old-fashioned editor to review your manuscript thoroughly. This would be someone with a track record, an outstanding command of the English language, an expert reader, and someone who appreciates the genre you're addressing. Such editors do not have to discover every typo. What you need them for is their reaction to your style, content, and delivery. When your publisher's editor delivers his edit, hand it over to your chosen editors. Let them look at it before you make any rewriting decisions.

If your publisher's editor has significantly marked up your work, then again, you should go over it with your chosen editor and evaluate it calmly. Take what is helpful, and ignore the rest. You, not they, are going to have to live with the legacy of this work.

You will also need your own copyeditor. Make this someone different from your line editor: This is a different sort of professional who will anally inspect all your punctuation, grammar, and spelling, without commenting on the content of the piece.

Some publishers still employ competent copyeditors—typically, they freelance the work out. If you work with one who is very good, get a name and request the same person for your future copyediting. But you cannot count on this. By the time the publisher sends you a proofread galley, time will be of the essence. You must be prepared with your own resources.

How You Can Spot an Incompetent Copyeditor
- You find more typos than they do.
- They use their red pens to scrawl long diatribes in the margins about their political and social arguments with your work. Examples: "Sting is the greatest rock and roller ever," or "Children shouldn't receive more sex education in the schools."
- When you quote famous authors, they "correct" those lines, no matter how famous those words may be.

Marketing

You must brainstorm with your advocates about what kind of marketing plan you'd like to see for your book. Will you be touring? Can you do satellite radio? Where is your press list? Do you have your own personal E-mail contacts? There are a lot of things to consider (see Part VI. Selling It, for more details).

You need to bring a marketing plan to your publishers, and you need to push for their commitment to as much of it as possible. The more your publisher works promotion, the less overhead for you, the less alone you feel in your efforts. Even if you're dismayed by their publicity department, or realize that your book has a very low priority, you have to think of it like this: It's your money or their money. Each of you alone does less than both of you together. They are already getting 90-plus percent of the royalties from your book; they can invest the time and money to get this going—you light the fire and keep it hot.

If your advance is under $100,000, the only thing most large publishers will be up for is sending out a press release, with copies of your book, to a list of people who might review it. They will put it in their catalog to booksellers. They will inform their sales force about it. They will not press for television coverage, and they will not woo contacts over the phone. They won't necessarily prepare a full book tour. The money they would spend on that might not justify what they paid for your advance.

If you received more than a $100,000 advance, you can expect more. They will try TV, they will make some phone calls, they will arrange a book tour. They might send advance copies to booksellers, and they might make special presentations to their sales force about you. They will urge you to give them creative ideas about how to market your book. They might even want to advertise, if they get excited by your advance-order numbers from the booksellers.

But again, it's a gamble. By the time their new season's books are coming out, they've already placed their bets. They'll put most of their time and energy into what they perceive to be the likely winners, which might be one, two, or three titles.

Are you in that golden circle? You certainly can't count on it. You can't count on promises they made when they were courting you, way back when the ink wasn't dry on the contract—when they said that you were going to be their biggest star, their highest priority.

If marketing plans are not in your contract, spelled out in black and white, then you cannot count on anything. Today's big-time publishers typically say, "We never put marketing plans in a contract, that would be suicide for us, we can't commit until we see how the book turns out."

What Have You Done for Me Lately?

But there is competition from print-on-demand publishers, from the new small book companies, and from self-publishers—the new technology of the book trade—and this is pushing big-timers to reconsider their contracts. I've already signed my first book deal that includes marketing commitments, and I'm sure it won't be my last.

When authors have something that others covet, they should feel bold to ask for what they need to ensure their book's success.

What if it all goes terribly wrong? What if your editor flat-out refuses to publish your finished work, or places conditions upon its acceptance that you could never accept? This is a nightmare that must be considered, because it happens all the time.

A friend of mine, "Clarissa," turned in a manuscript last year, after two years of writing—a memoir acquired by a prestigious editor at a prominent New York publishing house. The editor had already shown off Clarissa to all her friends in publishing. She was hot; she was the next golden girl! Her ears had burned with all the compliments she got on her incipient star power.

Two months after submission, her manuscript was returned with a terse note from her editor: "Not acceptable." After authors give up their lives to write a book, such a message can only leave them gasping for air. . . . Why would they do this? What could be "unacceptable"?

Welcome to publishing. Clarissa had to beg before she got any explanation at all. Finally, she got a note: Her story was too sordid. They hadn't realized her sexual career had been so down and dirty.

Now, as an innocent bystander, you might think, "Oh, New York publishing is sex-phobic; they aren't ready for realistic lives and honest sexual descriptions!"

But you would be wrong. The editor who gave Clarissa this critique made her career possible many years ago by publishing books that described every steamy liaison you can think of. She could give a fuck about "sordid" anything.

My friend's book might be flawed; I don't know, I didn't read her manuscript. I know that she had the chops to get a big-time book deal in the first place; but I also know that she, like most authors in a publisher's stable, is disposable. There are forces at work driving their decision on her book that she will never be privy to.

This is what we do know, those of us who have spent time in the

Big Time: You will never get a straight or credible answer from your editors about what they think of your manuscript, and you will never know what behind-the-scenes politics are driving their behavior. This very personal work of yours, created from your personal imagination and sacrifice, is destined to be dealt with in a very impersonal manner.

If you must have insight into why publishers turn down stories, kill contracts, and flush money down the toilet, then you should turn down the volume on the phone call from your editors and turn to the stock pages of today's newspaper. Those numbers will tell you more about the condition of your manuscript than anything that is being said to you or your agent.

The same caution is valid even if you are getting positive feedback. The publisher says they "love" your manuscript? You have to realize they might not have even read it. *Love* is not a word that has any meaning in this environment. Your editor's opinions about your work are irrelevant, whether they are complimentary or insulting. What you can find out from editors is your release date and production deadline—what they have done and what they are doing next. You are interested in their actions, not their reactions.

Every once in a while, you might meet an editor who genuinely seems touched by your work, who has a great love of literature, who yearns to talk with you about important ideas, and who seems personally invested in your success. This is so special, you'll want to involve this person in the rest of your career, wherever he or she ends up or whatever you might write.

If such people are competent, their special attention to you might get them in trouble. Their bosses might not approve of how they're spending their time on you. They're not supposed to confide in you; that's against the rules. You have different positions at the bargaining table, and that will inevitably reflect your rapport until one of you changes seats.

Rather than spend hours wondering and wringing your hands,

you should rearrange your priorities. You need to assemble your own team of advocates, editors, and marketing brainstormers. Let them deal with your editor and publisher in every case that you possibly can. Careless remarks from editors can ruin your whole writing day—don't even give them a chance. There's no way you can be tough-skinned enough to be indifferent to their offenses, so build your firewall and get behind it, pen in hand.

You need to write your book—they need to produce it and sell it, with your enthusiastic assistance. When you deal with them, you're a small business talking to a big business, not an artist talking to a mentor. Take the money and the time that they allow you, and invest these as if they were your very last dollar and your very last hour. With high hopes, and low expectations, you might be pleasantly surprised.

Small Press Publishers

The difference between large corporate publishing and small press publishing is much more than numbers, although the numbers do dictate the tremendous contrast in practices.

Small publishers are essentially bootstrappers. They have to carry the ingenuity, flexibility, and do-it-yourself philosophy to its maximum potential, or else they're out of the game altogether. They know that the big publishers have got national distribution markets sewed up. The only way they are going to get into a chain bookstore in a suburban shopping mall is to have an absolutely killer idea that no one else has thought of yet. Then they'll have the muscle to attract a nationwide distributor. They need guerrilla marketing to make a remarkable book known throughout the country. Their marketing creativity, and the ability to exploit a niche that the large publishers have not captured, are at the core of keeping their business afloat.

Erotic publishing is the perfect example of how small presses have triumphed with something that was too "hot" for mainstream publishers. When I started the *Herotica* series with Down There Press, in 1987, we had already tried every publisher in the country.

So Joani Blank published our book herself, at Down There Press, which until then had only produced sex education books. We published a collection of authentic, explicit, well-written erotic stories by women; as everyone knows by now, the books were a smash hit with both genders.

Down There Press had a bestseller because it was quite literally the only publisher on the planet willing to take the risk. It had the skills, from Joani's career in sex education and psychology, to understand "sex books." Joani also had a built-in "focus group"—the customers of her store, Good Vibrations—we knew what our customers wanted. We had a big mailing list, so we could contact every one of our customers directly.

Another example: My 1990 breakthrough book, *Susie Sexpert's Lesbian Sex World*, was one of the biggest successes in gay publishing. The title alone brought lesbian books out of cold storage. It, too, was an unlikely pick by a small press that believed in something no other publisher cared about.

Small presses have the luxury and the necessity of believing in things. Unlike big-time publishing, where subject matter is rarely a matter of anyone's personal taste, the whole point at small presses is what the publisher personally finds interesting. Small publishers are individual people who may well do the editing, proofreading, designing, and marketing. They may well stand next to the printing press when your book is in production.

Cleis Press, originally a two-woman operation in Pittsburgh, published feminist and lesbian books in the early 1980s, and they read my monthly sex columns in *On Our Backs* with undisguised glee. They liked it when I wrote about angry ex-lovers cutting up and melting their beloveds' dildos, or my escapades while running a fisting workshop at a Holiday Inn.

At that time, in 1990, big publishers weren't interested in lesbian anything; they could barely pronounce the word. But the multitude of feminist presses were also turned off—they believed my work was too renegade, and too patently offensive to most dykes, ever to have an audience of more than a handful of whores and punks. They were indifferent to the fact that I was selling 10,000 copies of our magazine every issue, and that I had a built-in publicity machine that toured the country. They didn't like the book, period—and as I said before, small presses make decisions based on what they, as individuals, like.

Cleis's passions—lesbian sex and lesbian family issues—ended up coinciding with excellent timing on the book market. My book came out in the early 1990s—when lesbians were coming out of the closet en masse and a new generation of dykes was impatient with their feminist foremothers' ideas of what was politically correct. The new lesbians wanted to be out; they wanted to be cool; they wanted to be sexy. They also wanted to have kids and to create their own tribe. My books, and other hot new authors that Cleis promoted, gave them the opportunity to hire a staff, have a real office, make new distribution deals, and ultimately move to San Francisco.

And what did those newly discovered and popular authors do? We did our next books with major New York publishers—because they offered us substantial advances and even better distribution. This is what happens all the time to small presses that are successful. They are like the minor leagues; they have to suffer the fact that whenever they take writers to the top, those people are ultimately going to leave them to get a far better deal. If successful small press authors don't take the next step up the ladder, not only will they shoot themselves in the foot financially, but they also won't be valued as much by their former small publishers. The small publishers might not like it that their star authors move on, but they aren't fools—they know the authors will go where they can make a living at writing.

When I wrote my book for Cleis, I worked full-time jobs elsewhere to support myself. Small presses can't pay you to write your book. They can only offer you token (or zero) advances, and take your finished product to market. Small presses rarely offer authors better royalties than large publishers; so even if you do have a breakthrough success with your book, you're still going to see your payment in small allotments for years to come. If your small press is financially unstable—and believe me, that goes with the territory—it might go out of business altogether, or find itself unable to make regular royalty payments.

Nevertheless, small publishers are likely to have a track record that is enormous compared to a first-time self-publisher. You could learn a lot from them—and sell an impressive number of books.

Benefits of a Small Press

1. They often have very literate, competent editors. You can decide quickly for yourself by asking for copies of books they've line edited. If you find a publisher you admire, he or she will be editing your book for you. You will not only save yourself the money of hiring an editor—which, remember, I said you must do with a large publisher—but you will also be mentored by someone whose skill you esteem.

2. You will have an instant core of fervent supporters, a group of people who are rooting for your cause. This small press picked your book because they believe in it, they think it's important, they got "personal" about it. If they give you a small advance, even a few hundred, or a thousand, dollars, it's a tremendous morale boost for your endeavors, in addition to gracing your pocketbook.

3. The small press has some media contacts, some media skills—and if you have none, you could learn from them. Think of yourself as their marketing intern. Unlike big publishers, who don't have the time or inclination for guerrilla marketing, your small publisher is keen on thinking of every crazy angle that could be acted upon.

4. The small press isn't making a fortune—in fact, they could be losing one—but what's pertinent to your case is that their cadre is running their own business, every nut and bolt. You are not going to have three different editors over the course of your book deal.

They don't even have the money to install a revolving door. Their staff, small as it is, tends to have less turnover, because ultimately the bosses themselves are running most of the show. You might crave that stability and personal investment.

These are all good reasons for choosing a small press contract, but unfortunately, they are not the reasons that most authors choose small publishers. Most novice authors go with small presses for very sentimental, irrational reasons that are going to cause them a lot of heartbreak in the future.

Major Small Press Myths

- ### They're the Only Ones Who Want Me

Being an unpublished author is like being the wallflower at the high school dance who can't believe anyone would ever ask her out on the floor. It's a *Carrie* waiting to happen, even if it never seems like that in the beginning.

When you think someone wants you, you're so flattered that you forget that your own interests are at stake. At various critical points, your career will deviate from that of your publisher's. The publisher is not your mom, your best friend, or your lover, and they don't even have the psychological wherewithal to avoid those comparisons . . . so you have to do it. Stop the transference!

If one publisher wants you, it means that something about the commercial viability of your project is self-evident. So it's likely that someone else will notice you too; in fact, having one suitor already improves your hand. Your second offer might be better; or you might decide that self-publishing is more appropriate.

It's always a rush when someone makes you an offer—and you can let them know how flattered you are. But you are not their servant or their son, you're their prospective talent. Are they right for you? Are you a good match? What is their very best offer? Is it the right time?

- **I Know They'll Always Be Straight with Me**

You need to get over this whopper in the next five minutes. "Small" does not equal ethical, honest, or dignified. Small publishers can cook their books as easily as big ones; they can hide the truth from themselves, and from you, as well as Rupert Murdoch can.

Small presses are frequently under hideous financial pressure. Paying you, one little person, is much easier to put off than paying their utility company, their landlord, or their insurance. They know that the typical author does not have an attorney on retainer, or an enforcer patrolling the streets.

I'm not excusing any small press malfeasance, I'm only explaining the forces at work that often create such situations. It's the same kind of heartbreak that a lot of friends and lovers go through when they assume, just because they're crazy about each other, that their financial concerns and practices are in agreement. Make no such assumptions!

You must have a written contract, and you must engage a professional attorney or agent to review it for you. This you can do for a flat fee. If you can engage an agent to negotiate for you, so much the better. You must insist on prompt and complete royalty reports. The publishers have to understand that they are dealing with you as a business, not as a darling writer with her head in the clouds.

You must insist on the same accountability with your publisher that you would with anyone you went into business with. Under extreme pressure, the only reason they will pay you what you're owed is if you can put them under worse pressure if they don't. Your contract and your professional conduct have to have some teeth.

- **We're Doing This Together for Our Community, Our Cause**

Pathetic, right? Only bleeding heart losers could possibly fall for this one, correct?

Yes, it's sad. It sucks so hard that this is one of the biggest reasons why I published the way I did for my first few books. Instead of telling you how ashamed I am, how foolish I feel, or the incredibly dumb terms I agreed to—all in the spirit of changing the world—let me tell you something else.

I think my personal passions—to make the sexual revolution personal, to provoke politics at their erotic core—are among the best things about me. What I needed to learn—and what you will, too, if you are gregarious, nurturing, or rebellious—is that your publishing contract is not the place where you're going to save the world.

Go ahead, write a book that sends your followers pouring into the streets, foaming at the mouth. Speak out publicly and often. Give to people who need it.

Your publishers do not need the shirt off your back; their profits are not going to fund the next revolution. They are going to take the money they make and use it for their next book projects, for their offices, and for their personal salaries. Even when they give their pro bono time and money, they are not going to ask for your guidance—they'll make their own decisions.

Save your generosity, and place your passion where it will do the most good. Believe me, your dreams are not in your royalty agreement. Think like a Marxist, not like a martyr.

- If I Have a Hit, I Could Make a Lot of Money with Them

There is virtually no way that this can happen unless you radically renegotiate your contract. Why not? Because the laws of small press physics are not set up to make it possible. If you have a hit, you might make a lot of money *later*, with someone else, but not with your original small press.

If the demand for your book *How to Fold a Sexy Napkin* is enough to make it a *New York Times* bestseller, your small press will not be "big" enough to handle the distribution and publicity—they literally can't grow as fast as a bestseller does. They will need to make deals quickly with bigger companies to handle their printing and distribution needs. When they do, they will be licensing your work and slicing up the pie in such a way that you will never get the lion's share of your work's value. When your book gets licensed, you get 50 percent of the sale, or 30 percent, or even 0 percent if that's what your contract says!

My first book series, *Herotica*, was a huge success, and my publisher sold the paperback rights—the book only comes out in paperback—to a large publisher, Penguin. My subrights deal was so weak that, instead of making 10 percent royalties on the cover price, as I did with the first *Herotica*, I make between 2 percent and 3 percent on *Herotica 2* and *Herotica 3*.

When I signed those contracts, I thought, "Oh boy, Penguin will sell so many of these, I'll get a tremendous reward for my work."

Yes, there have been oodles of Penguin sales; their distribution network is much bigger than that of Down There Press. They got their books into those shopping malls and airports. But I personally make more money on my original small press book, because I get a larger cut of the book's net income.

Let's look at an easy math model as a theoretical example: If I make $1 a book as a regular royalty, I will find that amount radically reduced by a licensing sale where my share is only, say, twenty-five cents per book. If the new edition sells 10,000 copies in one year, that's only $1,500, whereas my normal royalties would have made me $10,000.

I learned my lesson over a period of years. Over time, with less sales, I've made more money from the first *Herotica* edition that Down There Press held on to than I have from *Herotica 2* and *3* combined.

As you publish books over your writing career, you will come to depend on continuing royalties and licensing fees as a way to support you through lean times, or even when you need to expand your family or business. You will not think it is "cute" that you were idealistic

and foolish about your early contracts. You'll wince when you see
the numbers of your sales and realize that your contract didn't provide for your long-term success.

Save Yourself

There's been quite a bit of publicity about the phenomenon of older
blues musicians—the original rock 'n' rollers—who are impover-
ished because their original producers sold out to big record companies. Somehow the millions of dollars in profits never trickled down
to them. Several conscientious pop stars have raised a ruckus about
this scandal, saying that these pioneers should be compensated as the
treasures that they are, not thrown on some Medi-Cal scrap heap.

But pop stars like Bonnie Raitt and her pals are unfortunately not
available to you, the forsaken author, to kick your publishers' asses
and make them do right. We don't have any saviors for authors; we're
an unorganized mess.

But you could do right by yourself the first time. I've made small
press contracts since I wised up, and I've seen the positive results:
higher advances, fairer subrights deals, creative authority over my
work, and accountability. I've used agents and lawyers who were interested in working on small press deals. Living with the results of
your efforts to reach an equitable contract means you'll be able to
say *"Je regrette rien"* and have enough money to raise your glass.

Self-Publishing and the Internet

Self-publishing—the technology of desktop publishing software, E-books, and Print on Demand (POD)—is the current revolution in the book and magazine business. Most industry veterans have commented on its commercial, moneymaking potential; more profoundly, it is the most dramatic development in democracy and freedom of speech since Gutenberg's printing press. And like the advent of the printing press, the new medium has attracted sexually provocative work above all other kinds of expression.

Self-publishing is a creative dream come true. It removes the financial obstacle that keeps so many people quiet. Nevertheless, the new technology includes a business challenge that is like the triathlon of the publishing business: You're going to be doing every mile on your own, in every position, until you hit the finish line.

The relative ease of financing these kinds of publications has made some people forget that nothing else about it is easy. The chutzpah and single-mindedness that are required for self-publishing will make you wonder if your next stop should be Broadway or the World Wrestling Federation. Self-publishing is not for Tammys!

Self-publishing does not mean that you have to do every single thing all by yourself—just most of it. What you don't do, you pay for out of your pocket; it's your bottom line every step of the way. You write the story, and you assume the financial burden for producing it—as well as enjoying its profits, if you have some success. There's really nothing more to it than that, but that's enough.

Money is certainly the biggest reason that otherwise natural self-publishers have been held back in the past. It's been an obstacle that was once thought insurmountable—and all of a sudden, it's evaporated with the click of a mouse. Publishing on your own has now become so financially reasonable that even taking on a newspaper route, or cutting back on your ice cream budget, can allow you to save enough money to create your own book, Web site, or 'zine. If you have more disposable income on your hands, then you can build your own publishing empire at lightning speed, and with a relatively cheap cash outlay.

My mentor in Internet-savvy self-publishing is M. J. Rose, and she has written a book with Angela Adair-Hoy (my first E-publisher) that is a dollar-by-dollar, page-to-page manual of how to publish your own book and actually get it into the hands of a grateful audience. It's called *How to Publish and Promote Online*, and if you're attracted to self-publishing, you should read their book as if it were your first flight manual.

Rose was inspired to do a guide for self-publishers because her first novel, an erotic mystery called *Lip Service*, became the first E-book bestseller to "cross over," first at Amazon, and then in brick-and-mortar bookstores. I was just one of several thousand people who heard through the on-line grapevine that there was a wonderful new erotic novel that was self-published and becoming a sensation—I soon nominated it for *The Best American Erotica 2001*.

Who's a Self-Publisher?

Self-publishing is not for those who dream of riches from a winning lottery ticket. You will work your butt off to publish your book. The process requires authors who can take their already well-developed work ethic and turn themselves into a bit of a monster.

When you self-publish, you will neglect other things—like your health, family, and love life. Your naughty little secret will be that you aren't just running scared—you actually like this kind of life, this micromanagement of your publishing career. You won't just have insomnia from worrying—you'll also be awake in the middle of the night with some incredible new idea that you can't wait to act on.

The most difficult challenges I've had with self-publishing have been to protect my health and my time with my family. If I weren't a mom, with a powerful drive to be involved in my daughter's life, I might have lost contact with most of my personal friends and family by now. If I didn't have a partner making good meals for me every night, I'd be chewing on Baby Ruths and cursing my computer. At 10:00 P.M., I'd be on the phone, raving to some supplier, still wearing the bathrobe that I hadn't stepped out of since that morning. Birthdays and major holidays would pass me by in a haze of guilt and annoyance.

Self-publishing is not for the modest, nor is it for people who'd rather be behind the scenes, helping someone else. It's not the writing that makes it so, or the production. The noble part of self-publishing is creating the book; the daunting challenge is to market your creation once it's complete. You don't want to face your garage piled up with unsold books collecting dust and regrets. You have to be a literary exhibitionist. You have to be a networker, a blabbermouth, a media pig. You have to be tireless at connecting with every single person who shows an interest in your book. You have to believe that your book is the single most fascinating topic in the world—at least for your launch.

Marketing your writing is also a physical task. You'll want to travel the country. You'll make media calls at 5:00 A.M., and do book readings at midnight. The only thing that will keep your movie-star-size ego going is that you're passionate about your book. You never doubt that what you're doing matters.

Thinking like a movie star will help you no matter where you publish, whether you're at Random House or a small publisher. But when someone else is publishing, you can be a bit retiring, a little less obsessed. You can say, "Someone else is doing this job," and go to bed. But self-publishers are insomniacs.

How I Started Self-Publishing

My first self-publishing effort was in the technological Stone Age, in the 1970s, when I worked with a group of friends to publish an underground high school newspaper, *The Red Tide*. We wrote each of our stories with a pious demand for world revolution in the final paragraph, and we found sympathetic adult typesetters who would donate their time to our cause. We stayed up all night with a hot waxer—laying out our newspaper by hand, cutting out photos we liked from books or newspapers, and pasting everything down.

The Red Tide was, by turns, ridiculous and amazing. It was a startling surprise for our peers, parents, and teachers to see teenagers writing frank accounts about sex, drugs, and academic tracking by class and race—not to mention our political critiques of Palestine or Vietnam. Nobody thought high school students were that smart, radical, or sexually active, and we soon landed in a media spotlight. Many "grown-ups" gave us the tools and resources we needed because we were so precocious.

The Red Tide never published many copies—I wonder if we ever cracked the 5,000 barrier. Yet we were debated on nightly television; we were the subject of constant editorial speculation by the daily papers. We spent years embroiled in a free speech lawsuit against the L.A. Board of Education. Local right-wing fanatics were positive that our articles on birth control were responsible for the entire decline of our generation.

Our passion was politics, not journalism, and publishing was a tool to stir up our ideas. I didn't think a lot about professionalism at that time, but I remember how excited I felt each time a new story of mine was published. I treasured making a connection with every new sixteen-year-old who read it. We kept a mailing list of every reader and sympathizer we met, and I still have that list—it's actually a list of everyone's parents' homes. I planned to call them all one day and tell them when "the revolution" was at hand.

Little did I know that I was learning the basics of marketing, promotion, and sales while agitating for my anticapitalist cause.

You Own the Erotic Means of Production

Sexual expression has been the most persistent driver of every new expressive technology. What was Thomas Edison's first movie? A kiss! Why do we have VCRs in every living room? Because a bunch of horny guys wanted to watch porn movies at home. Why is the Internet the biggest erotic information medium in the world? Because some geek at the Defense Department took a break on-line one day, messing with the first generation of E-mail, and typed a revolutionary message: "What are you wearing?"

Today, with POD publishing, books can be cheaply printed one at a time. Anyone with a Kinko's nearby, or a home office, can control the means of production. You don't need to store an inventory. With E-books, there's not only no inventory, there's no freight, and your cut of the book price is up to ten times higher than a typical royalty. Your idea doesn't have to be adored by millions; in fact, screw those millions! You can reach, and profit from, a niche audience, regardless of whether other publishers think your stuff is esoteric, taboo, or out of fashion.

I first self-published this book as an E-book. I spent about $2,000 to produce it; I made that back in one month. I marketed it entirely on the Internet, and I went into the black at five weeks. I sold the book club rights, and then attracted the interest of Simon & Schuster, who could bring this book to millions of people's attention. I was able to make money, and get dozens of letters of feedback from readers and colleagues, from essentially pushing the send button on my E-mail software. Yes, I had a core of readers who knew me, but what surprised me was how many of my sales were to people who'd never heard my name before, they just wanted to learn about this subject.

Erotica is frequently about what other people "don't understand." Self-publishing and effective marketing allow you to cultivate a devoted, unapologetic milieu of people who "get it," who don't need you to be on the cover of *Time* magazine to be of interest.

All your audience needs is to find out that you exist. This means that your powers of seduction and attraction must be mighty. Don't think anymore: "Do I want to self-publish?" Think: "Do I want to be a star in my own universe?" If the answer is yes, then by all means, begin with due gravity.

The Literary Agents

Yes, you need an agent—if money and your writing career start having anything to do with each other. You need a publishing advocate to be your David against Goliath, to be someone who knows things you don't ever want to know, a champion who can sell for you and defend you and protect you while you sleep.

On the other hand, you have to think of your scale. There are authors who don't get an agent until they get a deal; there are authors who use entertainment attorneys to negotiate contracts; there are authors who handle every detail of their business themselves. The last are in a distinct minority. If you're writing as much as you should, you don't have time to be a full-time agent. So which job are you going to take?

The Lady or the Tiger

Some authors personally enjoy the negotiating process, the sales, the marketing, the arguing and schmoozing. I like some of those things myself; in fact, I've often whiled away the hours making all sorts of clever plans about how I was going to sell my book when I was supposed to be writing it!

That's the point: Writing is the ultimate labor-intensive activity. You have to do it; there's no squirming away. It's your story the reader wants, not your sales sheet.

So decide what you want to be. If you want to be a great agent, go for it; a lot of writers will love you like they've never loved anyone before. But if you want to be a writer, then get off the phone, get back to your dungeon, and *write*.

How Do I Become Agent-Worthy?

You won't necessarily feel the squeeze to employ the services of an agent until you've got a serious contract. But when you receive a fifty-page contract of largely incomprehensible jargon in the mail from your publisher's law firm, you'll start to get the picture of how much is at stake. Selling onetime magazine or periodical contracts might be simpler and shorter, but if you're successful enough, you'll want the same kind of advocacy in magazine negotiations that you'd expect on a book deal.

If you're a novice, don't start fretting about an agent from the beginning. Send your material to an editor at houses that actually look at unsolicited manuscripts—there are many small and mid-size presses that fit that description, as well as university presses. Publish your stories in magazines, journals, and on-line. Develop your own Web site, self-publish. Show that you have what it takes to put out work, quality work, consistently. Get noticed. You don't have to do everything on my list, but your creativity and your credibility have to be established by exposure. First you set up the lemonade stand; then your first agent, and your first book deal, will become possibilities.

With a solid book proposal or first draft in hand, you can approach agents. As much as it may feel as if you're auditioning for them, it's really just as much the other way around. If you've had some grassroots success and exposure, you've already shown your mettle. In the end, you're hiring them.

Agents have to know how to fight, and I do mean *fight*, for the best deals on your behalf. Their tenaciousness, knowledge, and devotion to your cause have to be pretty high. The author and agent have to impress each other mutually in order for the relationship to continue.

How to Find the Agent of Your Dreams

Agenting and talent management are a very intimate business. There's no line where you can queue up, like you're at a pizza parlor, and get a menu of talent to order from. Agents—good ones, and the good introductions to meet them—come through personal referrals and old-fashioned research. You can't hold out a tin cup. This is the "proving yourself" part.

> **Why Some Writers Can't Seem to Find an Agent**
> Would-be writers sometimes say to me, "I don't know any agents' names, not a single one!" This statement on their part tells me the following:
> - They have never read a book, or looked at the acknowledgments page, where they would often learn who authors credit their success to.
> - They don't look at credits of anthologies to learn where good stories have been originally published.
> - They have never read interviews with their favorite authors, where they talk about their influences and tell industry insiders' stories.
> - They don't go to writers' events—classes, workshops, readings, conferences—where there are loads of editors and agents, gossiping madly.
> - They don't interact, on-line or in person, with other writers—or if they do, they don't listen.

If you have managed to snag a book deal, it means that you've had contact with actual books, writers, and editors. You've been a good observer, listener, and student of how the world works. Already, you are impressive. The people you've met and cultivated in your apprenticeship are now happy to refer you to someone good.

The intimacy of an author with an agent is a mutual commitment. This is a match that will last considerably longer than your relationship with your book editor, or in many cases, your marriage. Because an agent makes a percentage of your royalties, you will literally be tied to this person even after you're dead. Find someone you like, someone who shares your attitude about books and the book business, and someone who inspires you. Talk to their other clients as if they were ex-wives.

Your Agent's Take on Erotica

Erotic writers sometimes worry about how their various publishers will take to their subject—will one be offended, or another titillated? There are so many voices involved in the publishing process that you will drive yourself mad if you try to anticipate them all.

Agents, however, need to be the people you can trust with this understanding. They should never be offended, or treat your erotic work like a joke or folly. If you realize that your agent is embarrassed or disdainful about your erotic writing, then you're not only getting a warning about their capacity to sell that work, you're also getting a clue that they don't understand the way you're creative, or why you're writing in the first place.

Make a formal agreement to work with your new agent on one project, or for a specified period of time. It's a probation period for both of you—to see if you like each other, and like the results. Show her your most provocative work; tell her the things you dream of doing. Find out if she knows how popular erotica is, and where the market is going right now for erotic writers.

You can afford the time to talk about this in the beginning, and even the small rejection that might come with it. When you do meet the right person, you'll have a partner and comrade through the decades of your creative and sexual evolution.

Part VI

Selling It

I'm an Artist, Not a Salesman

For as long as I've been talking to writers, I've been in the thick of arguments about how we're supposed to achieve our goals as artists when we're also compelled to act as our own advertisers.

Many writers feel that their brilliance as creative authors is incompatible with brilliant salesmanship. Some of us don't want to think about money—or are bewildered by organizational details. Others are profoundly shy in public. Some artists feel cheapened and alienated by promoting a "product." Some writers take to marketing easily at first, but then lose their way so thoroughly that when they come back to their writing desks, all their ideas are gone.

It's not a pretty picture. As much as writers get teased about our sensitivities—that we're spoiled, or oversensitive, or precious—our most paranoid fantasies are not too far from the truth.

Creative writing thrives on a certain amount of solitude and on independence from the need to satisfy the lowest common denominator. If we're interrupted, if we're constantly asked to shade our work to please the latest focus group, then our writing suffers. When we can't write as much as we'd like because of money worries, or when we write crap to pay the bills, then it gets harder to find the time to write well. A great writer isn't typically going to be a great secretary, bookkeeper, and salesman rolled into one.

Everywhere in the publishing industry, we see the rot of writers whose talents are squandered because no one promoted them, or because they were asked to write a book every six months until they

became blithering idiots, or because they were deemed media failures on account of their modesty and discretion. Even authors who
seek fame have often found themselves with an inopportune sound
bite or a dead-end reputation. Even the successful are saddled with
the Herculean task of reinventing themselves every year, to get one
more grab at the golden ring of public attention. The commercial
pressures on writing are virtually all bad news for writing itself.

You have two alternatives. One is to work at reviving the love of
reading—because the hardest task for authors today is to get anyone
to read at all. Your activism is needed immediately! Looking at the
big picture, the most important thing that I do to promote my books
is to read widely myself. I broadcast my recommendations to my
friends and fans, and my kid never goes to bed without a good novel.

Our competition as writers is not so much our peers as it is the
other media: movies, music, and the Web. How many people do you
know who are currently reading a book? How about yourself? I'm
including myself in this survey! I'm bewildered by all the media out
there, and I often don't know where to begin. I frequently find myself distracted by my newspaper and television. Every time I do read
a good novel, I think, "Why don't I do this all the time? This is my favorite activity!" But again, I find myself distracted, fighting for leisure
time to enjoy good stories.

Putting yourself in the reader's position, how do *you* find out
about a good new book? The best recommendation, of course, comes
from a friend whose taste you admire. From there, we tend to pick
up things that we've seen favorably reviewed or featured on a bestseller rack. If we go into a bookstore to browse, we might pick up a
book because the cover is so seductive. Maybe we have seen the authors speaking somewhere, and we decide to give their books a try.

You have to make your book known to others in the same manner that books become known to you. Whether you get your latest
reads from your mom, who mails you her discarded mystery novels,

or whether you just buy anything with a sexy cover that's mentioned
on the Banned Books list, you're responding to an act of promotion.

Most people aren't crazy about marketing. But unless you get a
charge out of filling a storeroom with all the unsold, unread copies
of your book, you're going to have to figure out a way to make your
work known. Yes, this takes an ego—you have to think that someone
besides yourself would enjoy your book. But if you're determined to
publish, then you must be equally determined to promote; the first
step is just a setup for the second. Your book doesn't have legs—but
you do, and only your efforts will get it into other people's hands.

Isn't This Someone Else's Job?

If other people are to do book promotion *for* you, they need to have
a considerable investment in the outcome. "Considerable" means different things to different people. Your publishers may have sunk several thousand into your project—but if they're a billion-dollar
corporation, they aren't going to treat you as much more than a tax
write-off unless your book succeeds like gangbusters. They're not being cruel; that's just the way their balance sheet operates. They are in
the gambling business, not the nurturing business.

What about a manager, a P.R. specialist, or your own private flak?
You can hire all those people, and you'll get exactly what you pay
for. Either you ask them to take as big a risk as you're taking, which
means they'll want to share some of the creative control—or else
you are funding their budget and supervising their efforts. I've
worked with some excellent promoters, but we've always worked
together, and it was never something I took for granted.

You might decide to turn to your family or best friends for help.
Again, how are their fortunes tied to you in this endeavor? Promoting a book is hard work. It takes dedication and enthusiasm; you

can't assume that true love will absorb all the stress and rejection that you're bound to encounter.

Scared Out of Publishing

Yes, I'm being deliberately grim in my list of demands on your time; I am the dragon at the bookseller's door. I'm sick of the commercialism, waste, and banality of book marketing, yet I have no advice to give you except that these are part of the dues you pay—on a regular basis.

Remember what I wrote in my Devil's Argument Against Publishing? There is honor in not going this way. If you insist on publishing, you're going to have to admit you're a glutton for punishment, just like the rest of us. Selling books *is* your job if you're writing books; you have to see it as just another way of telling your story— many, many times over.

My strategy for promoting my own books has been to devise a plan that is compatible with my life. There are a few strategies that all authors have to consider when they look for their audience, but you can interpret them in many different ways. Let's imagine your custom-made debut, which begins with your very own fan club.

Your Fan Club

Cultivating a fan club is my favorite part of going public. Who wouldn't enjoy a circle of supporters who really, really like you, who are thrilled to see your latest work? Your fans don't want to change one hair on your head, because you're perfect just the way you are! They offer you their beds, the last bite off their plates, the first taste of their private reserves. All they want is for you to keep writing!

Don't be a curmudgeon and tell me that you are immune to displays of infatuation. Even if you are a Grinch, your fan club would inevitably be filled with other would-be Grinches who adore you for your misanthropy. A fan club suits *you*, not the other way around.

Writing for the public is hard; it's largely an experience of indifference and rejection. You need a cadre of readers who think you're fab, because sometimes you can't quite muster all the confidence or spite you need to write for one more day. You need a cadre who will defend you, because that one critic who damns you can wipe you out for a year.

Maybe you don't believe me; maybe you think I'm weak for saying, "I ♥ My Fans." Go ahead, hold your nose in the air—but out of sheer necessity, you're going to have to build a fan base to promote your writing. Word-of-mouth, one-to-one recommendations are simply the strongest, most durable way to build a career in writing. Of course, they're also the slowest—you don't reach a million people at once, as you would with a TV spot—but they're the most permanent.

Readers who have been personally introduced to your work, who have met you, who have had even the smallest correspondence with you, are the ones most likely to read everything you ever wrote, and the ones who will pass your name on to everyone they care about.

I don't have an official "fan club"—there are no dues-paying members, no president, no innocent little boy band playing my theme song. What I do have is a mailing list (once on snail mail, now on E-mail) that I've been compiling for years. I write to everyone on my list whenever I have a new story out, or when I'm coming to visit their area—or even when I'm doing nothing in particular but I want to share my latest favorite sex toy, or rant about the latest news headlines.

I do have an official Web site, and this is by far the best aid to building my mailing list. Thousands of people hit on my no-frills home page every day, and every day some of them sign up for my mailing list. I would have to be on the road constantly to get even a tenth of the names I've collected on my Web site.

The Dawn of a Mailing List

But that's not how my mailing list started. A fan club starts with your personal phone book. You write to everyone in your life to whom you might send a holiday card or a birthday party invitation. In your first letter, tell your group what you're up to, and say that you'd like to stay in touch if they're willing to be on your list.

Of course, there will be those who decline—in Internet parlance, they will "unsubscribe." If you're talking about sex, you'll even meet those who profess to be shocked that they're on your mailing list, or who threaten you with legal action for harassing them.

In any case, your list will both grow and correct itself by natural processes.

Can you abuse your fan list? Yes . . . not so much by lack of attention, but rather by too much. If you want to post a daily diary and run it on your Web site, don't E-mail it out every day. Messages that are too long, or too frequent, dilute the occasions when you want to make a big impact. When your new book comes out, you don't want people to throw your message in the trash because they assume you're just complaining again about your flea-ridden cats.

Fans are great because you can try new ideas on them. When you ask them for feedback, they'll respond sincerely. They'll turn you on to new books and artists that you'll adore; they'll help you find a great bookstore to read in when you visit New York. They'll offer you a place to sleep when you're crossing Montana. Some of them will become friends, collaborators, mentors, and students. They'll jump out of cakes and write songs for you; they'll let you know, in no uncertain terms, that what you *wrote* changed the way they *live*.

Thank them, and then thank them again. Send a personal answer to all the people you can—and if that becomes too much, send out the most heartfelt form letter you can compose. Seal it with a kiss, and know that this is a love letter that's going to be treasured.

Performing Your Work

Shy people, this chapter is for you. After all, why do I even need to bother with coaching the hams? I'm a ham—I can barely print my chapter fast enough before I'm ripping the pages out of the paper tray, running downstairs to find an audience for my latest rant. I'm the one who told my last publisher I wanted to buy a bus and do a drive 'n' read tour of every coastal town from the Mexican border to the Canadian border. I've performed at strip joints, rock 'n' roll clubs, television studios, and baseball diamonds. I have the peculiar sensation that I can confide more intimately to a crowd than I can to a single person.

"Natural performers" don't need encouragement—they're off and running without a push. But shy authors are in a real pickle. They want people to read their stories; they need to find an audience in the multimedia thicket. But if they remain silent and unseen, only accessible within the pages of their book, they will be buried.

Your Internet Alter Ego

Luckily, technology is on the shy person's side. Today there are plenty of ways to seem as if you are a real loudmouth without ever actually making a live appearance. A personal Web site and mailing list will allow you to speak to thousands, and will allow a virtual facsimile of your presence. You can post photos or illustrations of yourself; or you can record your voice digitally, read stories on-line, or even manufacture a whole CD for your fans to listen to. If you get one of those Web cams that spontaneously captures your every move, you can be an exhibitionist and still be the only person in the room.

Interviews

Interviews on the phone, or face to face, can be difficult, even for the show-offs. What if you get an obnoxious interviewer—or, all too commonly, someone who's never read your work? You might even realize that they have no intention of printing any of their conversation with you; they only want some free sex therapy.

Once again, technology is on the shy person's side. E-mail and faxes will allow you to be a media darling without having to be put personally on the spot.

If Terry Gross from NPR begs you to make an appearance, or if David Letterman's people are calling you noon and night, then you, the shy person, might be faced with a real headache. But if they're calling you, you must be doing pretty well in the first place, so perhaps you can stick to playing the elusive star. Or maybe you'll want to get creative and ask to be interviewed without an audience—wearing a mysterious mask, or holding up cards and a Magic 8 Ball to indicate your responses.

TV Caveat

You're right to be concerned that making a bad, sweaty, Farrah-on-drugs television appearance will harm your career.

Television is the least forgiving media; it should be approached with full armor and your agent/manager in tow. Yes, TV does make you look fat. Perfectly reasonable hairdos and outfits end up photographing like a bad night at the homeless shelter. Weird tics and clumsy gestures you never knew you had can become the focus of the camera's eye. You could spend your entire five minutes staring at the wrong monitor.

A few strange creatures in the world are TV divas, and they need no guidance to make a stellar appearance. The rest of us mortals need all the help we can get to look good and appear somewhat coherent. Make a practice of getting copies of every one of your TV appearances so that you can critique them like a professional ballplayer. If you conclude that you're hopeless, you should raise a dignified white flag and accept no further offers to appear on the small screen.

Visual scrutiny is not nearly so awful in filmmaking. Filmmakers are interested in lighting you well—they want their audience to be enchanted with you. They have a considerably bigger investment in beauty and quality than the average TV talk show. You might not look "cute" in every movie, but you will probably be compelling.

With radio, of course, it's all about voice. If you have a nice one, you can show up in your pajamas and still knock 'em dead.

Live appearances are the most "naked" of all performances, but also the most beguiling. If you're just a little bit shy, but nonetheless willing, you should try doing a public reading. Your vulnerability and stage fright are part of what it takes to make that stage "charisma" that's so sought after.

If I'm not nervous before I take the stage, I know I'm not doing something right. It should feel like the big-time, like you're putting it all on the line—that adrenaline is alive and well inside your veins.

If you can acknowledge your fears and still go onstage, you'll have to revise your image of being a shy person. You're not truly shy; you're only eager to please and hungry to be adored. In that case, you can get right in line with the rest of us, hammy at last.

The Book Tour

Book tours are the most ambitious plans that authors can undertake to promote their work. Many writers would contend that a tour takes as much out of you as writing the whole book in the first place.

Is a tour really that inhumane—a virtual circus without the elephants? Yes, it's all that and more, but here's why people keep doing it: It makes geography work for you. The map of the world becomes your audience, no longer a hostile terrain. You will meet all those people in the world who "never leave the neighborhood." You will be an influence; you will be chocolate from the Aztecs, saffron from India. You, and your book, will have an impact.

On my first book tour, I had a five-month-old baby, and I went to fifteen cities in thirty days. I got stopped at the Canadian border and interrogated for hours because my luggage was stuffed with safe-sex accessories for demonstration. The customs officials suspected that the talcum powder on my rubber gloves was really cocaine. (My tip for entering Canada—avoid Toronto, embrace Montreal.)

My family came to "rescue" me when I got to my twelfth stop, New York, because I was having a bit of a meltdown. I lost my voice and got walking pneumonia. At the same time, whispering to my audiences in Brooklyn that night, I met people who told me they'd never been to Manhattan and didn't see any reason why they should go. But they came to see me, from California, so who knows what they might do next! A good erotic story could send them into orbit.

Planning the Tour

A book tour has two parts: the organizational stage to prepare it, where you are a general; and the foot soldier part, where you follow your pushpins around the globe.

First of all, you need to think about the scope and timing of your tour. You might only be able to tour your immediate region; you might have only three weeks to spare for this.

Don't despair if you realize you don't have three days for a book tour, let alone three weeks or months. Your forte will become virtual touring and getting great reviews—you won't be on the bus this time.

Another brilliant idea to make book touring affordable and practical is to share a tour with other authors. I have a relationship with a clan called Sister Spit, a group of women writers who get two slightly reliable vans every spring and summer and tour as many cities as they can, sharing expenses, planning, and all the glory. None of them could have done it by themselves, but their collective energy has made them headlines and regional notoriety all over the United States.

Make Your Scheme

The organizational part of planning a tour is a meticulous process in which you solve horrendous story problems like, "If I travel to Chicago from Davenport on a train going sixty miles an hour, can I do three media appearances and two store signings before the next red-eye to Boston?" (Answer: Airline fuckups and weather unpredictability trump "minutes available" every time.)

If you've ever been a "soccer mom," a legal secretary, a chess master, or an offensive line coach, then you might be good at organizing a book tour. You have to be fascinated with manipulating time, knowing when to strike and when to surrender.

If you have more time to travel, your audience connections will be better, your health will last longer, and you'll have more flexibility to accommodate all the possibilities. But a book tour is not a real job—no one pays you to go on the road, unless you're funding it by a continuous string of paying gigs. Whatever you typically do in your family life and your career, it all goes out the window while you're touring.

The book tours I've enjoyed most occurred when I was driving with companions, not flying. I spent up to a week in major cities and regions, and I always had the time to eat right, sleep well, and exercise. I had time with my family and friends; I also had troops at home feeding my cats. I don't think I've ever experienced all those good parts simultaneously on a book tour, but that's my goal.

The book tours I've regretted have been those stupid affairs where I flew in and out of a major city every day, and half my media gigs were canceled, or the bookstore I planned my whole gig around turned out not to have my current book.

One night I was stuck in Chicago, waiting out the weather problems at O'Hare, and my plans for the day looked bleak. I had been on the road for ten days, and I'd already lost my voice. Planning an emergency "steam room" procedure, I discovered that the hot water didn't work in my hotel faucets, and I started to cry.

Halfway through my bedside Kleenex box, I got a phone call from a pal of mine, Jefferson, who managed the rock band R.E.M. at that time. He told me that he was in Chicago that night as well, playing a gig, and offered me tickets.

"I don't want any excitement; I want a hot bath," I whispered. "I'm dying on this tour already, and we've barely started."

Jefferson was more sympathetic to me than I expected. I felt a little silly complaining about my minuscule book tour when I knew that he managed year-long odysseys of rock 'n' roll road trip insanity.

"But it's really all the same," he said, soothing me, offering me various hot water availability schemes. "You *are* the golden goose, and the moneymakers will try to kill you to get the last egg. Someone's got to protect the goose, because you're still going to be around long after all the little egg grabbers have gone on their merry way."

I advise you to heed his words. Yes, see America, plan a book tour for yourself. But make it a golden little tour where your feathers get stroked, not plucked. Be influential, prize your time with the new and unexpected, and don't forget the future waiting for you back at your writing desk, the nesting room to which you will eventually return.

Postscript for the Erotic Book Tour Traveler

Yes, you will get seductive invitations. People will want you at their parties, in their playrooms, between their rubber sheets. The younger you are, and the less sleep you need, the bigger your dance card gets. It's an immune system roulette wheel; but, of course, all the nice touching and affection, plus the odd orgasm or two, are at least as good as a bottle of vitamin C.

What you want to avoid, of course, are the nuts—the people who want to stagger you with their sexual performance, fall in love on the spot, and then discuss their latest manuscript in detail while they order up more room service on your tab. These are another variety of goose killers—be away with them! You'll be blindsided at first, but soon you'll see them coming.

The best groupies are the ones who do it all the time, the professional sex workers. They know you are depleted, and they graciously fill you up. They encourage you to be selfish, silly, cross-eyed. The best after-gig sex I ever had was with two goddesses who massaged every inch of my body and then tucked me in with extra blankets and a kiss on my brow before they silently slipped away. Always say yes to such muses, and if they spread your reputation far and wide, do the same for them.

The Reviews: Meet the Press

I am a compulsive book reviewer. Not only do I write reviews, but my opinions on books—and movies—are standard fare at any meal I'm interrupting, any class I'm teaching, any dentist appointment I'm trying to delay.

I'm glad I've been a professional book critic, because it's given me a valuable vantage point as an author seeking good reviews of my books. I understand the natural conflict of interest between journalists, who want to write great book reviews, and authors, who want to promote their books to impulsive shoppers.

A *great* book review, from a critic's standpoint, is one that exploits a book's premise to create a provocative new essay from the critic's viewpoint. For example, when I reviewed Catherine MacKinnon's book *Only Words*, it wasn't because it was an entertaining yarn or because I had much to say to her fans—or even that I was trying to give a fair synopsis of all her points. No, I wrote an essay called "The Prime of Miss Kitty MacKinnon" as an attack on what I saw as the hypocrisy and self-denial of antiporn feminism. It was a big success—reprinted in a dozen places, used in countless classroom discussions—but I bet hardly anyone remembers that it was a "book review."

I've done the same with books I loved. When I was a columnist for the *San Francisco Book Review*, I wrote about Elaine Brown's *A Taste of Power*—an account of her years as a member, and then chairman, of the Black Panther Party. In her case, I was favorably disposed to the book, but what made the "review" memorable was that I used Brown's subject to talk about the unspoken sexual politics of the left-wing organizations in the 1960s and 1970s.

The typical review that makes an author happy is called, in the journalism trade, a "service piece." This is writing that sells something, while supposedly giving consumers the help they're looking for. Service pieces are the life's blood of most of the magazines you see on the newsstand; they offer their corporate patrons an essential form of unpaid, but absolutely expected, advertising. The publishers won't get invitations to screenings, review copies of new books—let alone paid ads—if they don't cover the products of the entertainment world they're promoting. It's the quid pro quo of the magazine business.

Take *People*, for instance—a magazine in which most authors would give their eyeteeth to be mentioned. *People* does run negative reviews, but their main accent is on the positive, and they always want to have something to recommend. Even when they're not enthusiastic, *People* rarely employs outright condemnation. If the reviewer gets a little too honest and confesses, "This sucks!" the editor will write a softer headline: BETTER LUCK NEXT TIME! The author sighs with relief, even if you know the regular readers are deciphering between the lines.

Other service-style book reviews only serve to make fun of your book, to make the readers laugh or squirm. Erotic, for them, is the ultimate opportunity for a cheap shot.

I got a quickie review of *The Best American Erotica 2000* from the *Washington Post* that noted some titles, in brief, for summer reading. The critic said, "If you like it raw—Siamese twin kind of stuff—you'll find this to be hog heaven."

"I don't know if this is supposed to be a compliment," I said to my editor, "but it sounds like our book will give the readers trichinosis."

Let's take a look at the "Siamese twin" story that the critic refers to. It's a piece called "ReBecca" by novelist Vicki Hendricks, an author and professor of creative writing with a penchant for the noir genre. "ReBecca" was published in several magazines, because no editor who read the first sentence could resist it:

> As her Siamese twin joined at the skull, I know Becca wants to fuck Remus as soon as she says she's going to dye our hair.

The Siamese twins' story—their argument about their virginity and romantic ambitions, is explicit, yes, but also tender and anxiety provoking all at the same time:

> I think our bodies work like the phantom-limb sensation of amputees. We get impulses from the brain, even when our own physical parts aren't directly stimulated. I'm determined to do what [Becca] wants and not give her mind a chance to stop it. She follows along. We get into the bedroom and I set us down. Remus sits next to Becca. Without a word, he bends forward and kisses her, puts his arms around her and between our bodies. I watch.
>
> It's an intense feeling, waves of heat rushing over me, heading down to my crotch. We've been kissed before, but not like this. He works at her mouth and his tongue goes inside.
>
> The kissing stops. Remus looks at me, then turns back to Becca. He takes her face in his hands and puts his lips on her neck. I can smell him and hear soft kisses. My breathing speeds up. Becca starts to gasp . . .
>
> "You're beautiful," he tells her.
>
> "Thanks," I say. I get a jolt of Becca's annoyance . . .
>
> I wake up later and look to my side. Remus has curled up next to Becca with one arm over her chest and a lock of magenta hair spread across his forehead. His fingers are touching my ribs through my shirt, but I know he doesn't realize it. I have tears in

my eyes. I want to be closer, held tight in the little world of his arms, protected, loved—but I know he is hers now, and she is his. I'm an invisible attachment of nerves, muscles, organs and bones.

The *Post* review of "ReBecca" is filled with the kind of thoughtless, icky-poo comments that diss erotic authors every day. You get made fun of, you get put down for the very notion that you've dared to combine writing with sex: "If it's good art, it's isn't good porn." This parochial type of critical thought holds that good smut—because of its orgasmic result—cannot excel as prose. There's the entire mind/body split laid out to behold, a perfect aerial view.

Many press reviews of erotic work come with a wink and a nod— "If you're a horny loser, you'll love it"; "Raincoaters and lonely housewives, get a load of this one!" Of course, no one wants to pipe up and admit that he's a horny loser or she's a desperate housewife, so the damage is complete.

The Bestseller List

Authors obsess about bestseller lists more than any other critical determination, either following them religiously or vowing never to look at one again. But lists have transformed themselves today into a much more author-friendly and democratic institution. So many people over the years disputed *The New York Times* determinations that rebel lists started appearing in other daily papers. Bookstores decided they wanted to tout their own favorites. With the salon atmosphere of the Internet, everyone with a user ID started creating their own best-loved and top-ten listings. If you haven't composed and promoted your own top-ten list yet, what are you waiting for?

Authors of books should welcome and cherish any and all reviews. The most negative review you get might inspire a rebel reader to embrace you. The most inconsequential service piece might stick out in a book browser's mind the next time she goes shopping for soda pop, and she'll come back with your paperback in hand. The most eccentric top-ten list could be circulated like wildfire on E-mail and make you into an Amazon.com publishing star.

Those "great" reviews I talked about earlier can be infuriating to authors, but in fact they only appear rarely—when the subject of a book, or its creator, is considered weighty enough to have shaped our culture. I've been discussed in lots of weary articles that decry the spread of popular erotic writing; they conclude dismally that "Susie Bright" stands at the peak of a literary dung heap.

The very quote I've used to promote this book, from a *New York Times* reviewer who called me "the avatar of American erotica," was written by a man who thinks such erotica constitutes, on the whole, a rather awful development. Ah, but now his disdain is just another happy pull quote for me.

I hope Catherine MacKinnon has similarly reflective words to say about my early critical reviews that described her career. After all, I could have written about a dozen other more deserving antiporn activists, but no, I chose her! I bet I sold an awful lot of her books.

Part VII

Doing It

What's Going to Happen to Your Sex Life

There are two personal destinations that await every erotic author. One is your "sexy" image, which is guaranteed to be larger than life. The other is your sexual imagination, which will also grow to tremendous proportions—but which won't create nearly as much of a splash in the public eye as it will in your own mind.

The more common curiosity, as to whether you actually have more sex with more people, is uncertain. Your bedroom escapades may not change at all, despite your new reputation and creative capacity. Some bystanders will find it hard to believe—after all, if you have the capacity to arouse strangers through the written word, aren't you just as devastating in person? Don't you enchant your audience into complete submission?

Fame and Sex

If you're famous enough, through any avenue of celebrity, you will have people eager to go to bed with you. One big catch: You may not feel attracted to them. Like any tearful tabloid movie star, you may simply crave someone to like you "for yourself," rather than for the steamy rumors that your success has inspired. If you are commercially successful, you may wonder if people are being kind to you because they think it will benefit them professionally or financially—that's a definite anti-aphrodisiac.

My ten-year-old daughter and I saw a popular Hollywood movie called *Almost Famous*. One of the central characters, a rock 'n' roll star played by Billy Crudup, was a dead ringer for a boyfriend I briefly hooked up with in high school. It was a nostalgic surprise to be reminded of my old flame, and I confided to my ten-year-old that I had been chiefly attracted to my Crudup look-alike because he was so desirable among the other popular girls.

My daughter thought that sounded juicy, and she pressed for more details. "Oh, I'm cringing about it now," I said. "I never had any deep feelings for him other than to prove that I could seduce him. . . . Once I'd made my point, I didn't know what to do with him anymore. I wanted his 'image,' and once I had it, there was nothing left." This is what a sexy reputation gets you—people like me at sixteen, trying to prove something, or people who treat you like a symbol instead of an individual.

I *do* like the attention I get for my erotic writing—the social and political attention, the writerly kudos. But if you ask me about actual sex and my real-life lovers, it's a different story. I've never had a relationship with someone I met because of my writing or my erotic fame. The only people with whom I've felt truly uninhibited are those who've come to know me on a very different level than that of my writerly reputation.

As for one-night stands, I've honestly enjoyed them more with people who didn't have a damn clue who I was. If I succumb to a fan's seduction, we both inevitably end up feeling as if we're on some kind of performance test drive. That's not always awful, but it's "in the way."

The reputation of a being sex symbol is quite a mantle to carry. You don't have to be particularly famous to encounter it. If you're recognized even for one erotic story, people will assume you have a giant libidinous appetite, a sexual ego the size of Alaska. They'll speculate about whether you have a sadistic streak, a fetish drawer, a perpetually dirty mind. Whatever the speculators consider sexually perverse, they will enthusiastically project onto you. If your ardent fans are secretly obsessed with porn stars, they'll imagine you to be a virtual diva. If their fantasy is leather, they'll be bewildered by your flannels. You'll be astonished at the way you appear, over and over again, as the reflection of latent desires. It will provide great fodder for writing—but, alas, a real turnoff for your own sex life.

The Bigger and Better Erotic Mind

I said at the beginning there were two destinations for an erotic author. The first, your naughty reputation, is by and large a phony lark. However, the second result—the expansion of your erotic and creative imagination—is exhilarating and altogether to your advantage.

When you write erotica and write it well, you're entering an elite of writers, a cadre of talent who write about the most intimate, subtle, and dramatic of material. Your writing chops are going to go through the roof.

Because you will be observing and describing sex so closely, your sensitivity to what turns you on, and your empathy for what turns others on, is going to become ever more radarlike. You'll be able to read people's sexual psychology through observation, and it will change the way you look at the world. You'll pick up on the loneliness, the cravings, and the impending erotic explosions so keenly, sometimes you'll wonder if it could split you in two. With luck, your body will remain intact, but your characters will express these dynamics. You will become a literary expert on heat.

This "tuning in" to the sexual world is, in itself, erotic. Your fantasies will become infected with your vivid realizations. Your lover(s) will see a change in you. If you're satisfied with your present love life, it will be enhanced; if you're sick of it, your unhappiness will be a lot harder to hide.

For some erotic writers, storytelling is the dress rehearsal for scenes they are hungry to enact in real life. For other authors, the fantasy on paper is as good as it gets; they don't want to take it further. Real life, in their case, would be anticlimactic. I myself have felt both ways—daring and shy, exhibitionist and Walter Mitty–ish.

When I was young and had done hardly anything sexual—let alone experimental—I got all sorts of ideas from books, and I was eager to try them out. Years later, my feelings of burning virgin curiosity are not so common, but I have much more erotically satisfying relationships with my most implausible fantasies.

The Best Days

When I have a good day writing, it feels as potent as the hottest sex—literally, just as thrilling. My writing euphoria has its own peak. I haven't yet had an orgasm right at the keyboard, but if you'd touch my shoulder at the right moment, I'd probably shoot out of my chair. It's a rush, and one that I savor. When people ask me if my sex life has improved from erotic writing, I tell them that, actually, any old writing will do—and yes, it's the best I've ever had.

You Are a Sex Guru

When you write about sex, it's a little bit like stepping into a phone booth with your Superman costume. As you emerge with your spicy new story in hand, you'll be treated not only as a writer, but as a political activist, a Planned Parenthood rep, and a naughty Dear Abby, all rolled into one.

I was once on a radio show with two other women who, in one way or another, write about sex. The first was Candace Bushnell, author of *Sex and the City;* the other was Sherrie Schneider, one of the authors of *The Rules: Time-Tested Secrets for Capturing the Heart of Mr. Right.*

Candace's book is actually not about sex at all, but is rather a satire on the jaded lives of the Upper East Side singles set. *The Rules* is about getting married to someone rich enough so that you, too, can live a jaded life on the Upper East Side—I guess the satire begins after you get the ring on your finger.

I liked Candace's book—hated Sherrie's—but in our group interview, I felt sympathy for them both. Neither author is a "sex expert," yet they were being grilled as if they were Masters and Johnson.

The only explicit sex in Bushnell's book is in her title. *The Rules* ladies implore their readers to hold out on sex until after the marriage license is sealed and delivered. What the hell do they know about Andrea Dworkin's porn theories, or the latest herpes remedies, or connections between masturbation and spirituality? Probably nothing—yet because they are associated with a sexy topic, they can expect to be interrogated on every matter of human sexuality. At the very least, they will be asked such chestnuts as, "What makes a man good in bed?" and their opinions on penis size. Yet two writers such as these could be very shy on such subjects, or be honestly bewildered by such questions.

The point is, you don't have to know anything about sex—as science, culture, or politics—in order to write an erotic story. And you don't have to write erotica to be grilled about sex! Writing an arousing scene requires craft and imagination, but it does not mean you've taken the clitoral SATs. You might be very modest in public; you might be the last one among your friends to offer sexual advice. Nevertheless, you have as much right to compose an erotic story as any writer. But you need to be prepared for the possibility that, as of your first sexual word, you will become an erotic guru in others' eyes.

In the interview with Candace and Sherrie, Candace took the modest role. She didn't get as much airtime, but she didn't make an ass of herself. Afterward, I bet she got on the phone to her agent and said, "Never again." This is a woman who should be interviewed as a sort of Jane Austen for our times, not as the Happy Hooker.

Still, an author like Candace could set the boundaries. She could tell that radio show personality, "I like to develop every part of my character's lives, and their sex lives are important to my story—but I don't think of myself as a sex educator."

Sherrie, on the other hand, took the offensive. She got a lot of exposure, but she didn't come across as either sexy or wise. Her response to everything was, "Are you married; do you want to be married?" If you answered no, then she'd demand, "Then why am I talking to you?" If you answered yes, then she told you to swallow hard. She wasn't about to give one speck of her sexual opinion; she overrode those kind of questions with moral prescriptions.

I wished she would come right out and admit that she puts a low priority on female sexual satisfaction. But she might need a mickey in her drink to confess that.

I, on the other hand, relish situations where I get to address every shade of the sexual spectrum, because I thrive on all of it. Sex as history, as art, as biology, as politics—that's my favorite conversation. For me, sexual questions open up the world. Sex is my intellectual playground, and I suffer only when others around me don't take it seriously. If someone asks me about penis size, I'm going to talk about why I think masculinity and dick size are such a provocative topic of conversation, or about who most frequently asks that question. I could talk about it for hours . . . and I have.

I came to my "sex writing" through political activism and sex education. I like to teach; I like to be a busybody; I like to rattle the cage. I am friends with other erotic writers who also enjoy wearing the sex guru tiara—we're pretty unabashed about it.

If you're a natural-born teacher, there's really no problem with being dubbed a sexpert—it's all cake—except that you have to avoid going out too far on your limb of helpfulness.

For instance, I get letters from a lot of readers who ask me to advise them on particular sex dilemmas. Even though I often find their experiences very moving, I've realized that it's reckless to answer them spontaneously. Unless I'm their therapist, or longtime observer, I really have no idea how they're spinning their stuff, what's left out, or what I don't know. If I were crazy enough to write back quickie remedies—like "Divorce him!" or "Add salt!"—it would terrify me to be held accountable for the consequences. Instead, I usually send the following letter:

Thank you for writing me and getting to the point. If I am able to inspire or help you through my books and classes, I'm honored, but to be honest, I don't give personal advice outside my own family and friends.

I do feel reluctant to give you guidance, when I'm not your therapist, close friend, or family. It's so easy to misinterpret the letters I receive, or jump to conclusions.

I know you're not alone in this, and I'm hoping that you will find someone closer to you—a friend, counselor, or support group—who can give you more realistic feedback and fresh ideas. I'm sorry I cannot be of more personal help . . .

I do answer "personal" sex questions in the advice columns I write for publication, but it's like "Dear Abby"—I don't give personal replies, only public ones that are published. If someone wants to send a question to my advice columns, I forewarn them that I pick only one question a month to answer, which is hardly a substitute for personal attention!

The Naysayers

One of the most peculiar consequences of erotic writing is the way one is villainized for it. You may be a most rational person—utterly unconcerned with superstition, religion, or antiquated moral customs—but no matter. Regardless of your personal beliefs, you will feel the wrath of those who are offended. And I do mean *offended*. Your scientific mind or amused indifference will be mussed up, at the very least. At its worst, you may feel tremendous guilt and fearful regrets for the repercussions that touch your nearest and dearest.

The main thing that deters people from writing erotica publicly is their apprehension that their parents or children will see their work and suffer from its publicity. As long as that apprehension is alive, it can never be said that sex is no longer a taboo subject, or that it's all a big yawn to the oversexed masses.

Sex is not yet a yawn; it's still a soft squishy spot for all sorts of social persecution. Too many people are humiliated and discounted because some bluenose has painted a scarlet four-letter word on their reputations. In our new millennium, we are witnessing a peculiar double standard, in which erotic authors are deemed intriguing one moment and disgusting the next. We never know from review to review whether we're going to be pilloried or embraced.

Selling the Anti-Sex

Worst yet, there are whole periodicals that are devoted to racy, sex-filled editorials that state, in no uncertain terms, that everyone is sick to death of sex—and they'll say that every week as long as it sells papers. In fact, this "hip-crit" is the current state of American Puritanism. It's not cool anymore to say that sex itself is bad, but it's ever so smart to claim that sex is overdone and tedious. In an editorial for *The New York Observer*, called "Enough! The Overexposure of Sex Is Ruining the Mood for Everybody," writer Alexandra Jacobs writes:

> Sick of sex?
>
> You're not alone. But you'd be forgiven for feeling misunderstood in today's New York. The city has never been so giddily, aggressively sex-positive; some days, living here feels not unlike living inside the brain of a pubescent male: sex-soaked, but not sexy. A visitor from another part of the country might take a look around and conclude that New Yorkers are copulating and cyber-sexing their way into the new millennium. It's as if the peep shows were ripped out of Times Square, only to take residence in our collective psyche. One does not have to be a prude to proclaim, "Enough!" We have entered an era when sex has become so mainstream, so ubiquitous, so chintzy.
>
> [. . .] Have we perhaps come to a point where to have sex is to be complicit in something cheap and tacky and soul-destroying, like finding oneself trapped in an airbrushed magazine photo spread of "Hot Young Actresses"?

I would be more sympathetic to her criticism, except that you will never see a newspaper critic making a similar analysis about marketing trends in money, for example, or the search for the perfect romantic relationship.

If anything is "overexposed" and "soul-destroying," it has to be the endless coverage of financial excess. Similarly, clichés of romantic happiness, the perpetual marches to the altar, are not unlike being inside the brain of a pubescent girl.

Living with a "bad reputation" as an erotic man or woman of letters means that you are going to become an expert on hypocrisy. Nicholson Baker, author of *Vox* and *The Fermata*, told me he was amazed when some critics lauded him on one day as one of the best writers of his generation, but were ready to box his ears the next when they decided he was a smut peddler for writing such novels. Did he have a nervous breakdown and lose all his writing marbles when he wrote an erotic book? Of course not. But it was fashionable for some critics to bash his erotic work, to sell sex by loathing sex.

Protection from Prudes

Is there any way to stop being on the ball end of the puritanical yo-yo? Where do you find protection?

The first step, of course, is to feel proud of your work. If you think your sex writing is embarrassing, or inferior to your other work, then you are the proverbial sitting duck. I've talked with novelists who are pressured by their publishers to "spice up" their love scenes a bit—who are told that they need to get racier if they want to increase their sales. Such pressure should be resisted at all costs, unless you're thrilled to be asked. If you comply unwillingly, the readers and critics will inevitably begin to buttonhole you and demand an accounting for your racy transformation. It won't be your publisher who's answering the flak.

When I talk to writers who are reluctant to explore their erotic potential, I don't push them to take action; I hand them a brace to bar the door. Protect your privacy and your timing, because no one else is going to take on that burden.

The Latent Projection Machine

Enthusiastic erotic writers, however, will go forward with their work; along with the kisses and kudos, they'll take a few pies thrown in their direction. This is when one must revert to the kindergarten mantra: "Whatever you call me sticks on you and not me." Most criticisms of erotic writers will be of the most latent variety. Colleagues who say you're sick, perverted, and queer are the very people who have the most guilty analogous secrets in their closets. Stay in publishing long enough, and you'll probably see their coming-out parties—but don't expect any notes of apology.

Many of the people who "hate" you and your work behave ferociously because they mistakenly believe your work is prescriptive—that you're insisting that everyone follow your lead. I've had interviewers who were visibly nonplussed when I didn't show up for my appointment in rubber and high-thigh boots, because they were all ready to rail against my presumed S/M indoctrination. They want to rebel against you, the dirty writer, like children pushing away their bowl of cooked carrots. One can only presume how fed up their own mothers got with this kind of behavior.

Prudish critics will be surprised if you're intelligent, if you're thoughtful, if you refuse to rise to their bait. In fact, when this kind of critic confronts you with a negative sexual indictment, you must treat it as if he or she is making a confession.

I'm gentle with such accusers, because I know they're on the edge. When someone asks, "Don't you ever think about anything but sex?" I know this is someone who can barely think of anything else. "How can you defend bisexuality?" is only asked by those who are tortured by bisexual fantasies. "Isn't the American public sick of hearing about sex?" is a problem posed by those who are terrified about their sexual ignorance. I'm sure there must be some exception to my rule of the latent hostile critic, but I've never been let down yet.

Pseudonyms

You may wonder if using a pseudonym is the only way to protect yourself and your family properly. Be my guest . . . but understand that the first people who break the anonymity of pen names are the authors themselves. Why? Because it's very hard to never get any direct feedback or praise about your work when nobody knows it's "you." You might discover you have a bigger ego than you think, no matter how much of a milquetoast you've been mistaken for.

Authors always worry that it's their editor or publisher who's going to blab all over town, but I haven't found that to be the case. I've gone to elaborate lengths to disguise writers I've published, upon their request, to the extent of sending their fee in cash to a general delivery address. All too soon, I'll see these same secretive persons toot their horns on completely unprivate occasions.

Those who are able to maintain pseudonyms indefinitely are people who have full lives in other departments and who keep a great many details close to their vest. They invest a lifetime in keeping their secret, and their anonymity doesn't upset them. Anonymity is a burden—one that I certainly couldn't carry myself.

Your Comrades in Arms

There's nothing like a community of like-minded friends to lift your spirits when you are wounded. The best part of writing erotica today is that there's a bohemia in everyone's virtual backyard—whether you find it at a local café, or at a workshop, or on an Internet bulletin board. There are thousands of people who love to discuss sex, and the craft of writing, without sparing a breath for a single sacred cow or knee-jerk denunciation. The era of "shocking" people, in the gratuitous sense, is *over.* What's shocking now is authenticity, ethics, and a sensitive touch. Let yourself be amazed in sympathetic and fine company.

Sex Writer Burnout

One of the most curious questions people ask about sex writers is whether they have sacrificed all the juice in their sex life for the sake of writing stories to arouse others. Has our lemon been "squozen," and then frozen? Do we find ourselves dry, impotent, grasping at fantasies that don't have another drop left in them?

I get a kind of perverse glee in visualizing the spectacle of "sex jag": I believe it's a classic American mind-set about imagining punishments for self-indulgences that are yet to be committed. Our country spends a lot more time preparing for all the bad things that are going to happen to us because of sex than it does thinking about where the creative and sensual possibilities lie.

Still, if sex writing caused sex burnout, it would be my obligation to confess it to you here. Instead, I have another conclusion to offer: Erotic writing has never screwed up my sex life—quite the contrary.

However, formulaic writing *is* a creative burnout, and *that* is a libido killer. Writing to others' specifications, when they don't match your own, is exhausting. Repetition on demand is mind-numbing. This is the same whether you're writing about orgasms or widgets. Even the most sensitive material is bound to plague you if you don't get to explore it creatively and add some variety to your writing diet.

However, the professional world isn't set up for anyone's creative flowering. If you become well known for writing about anything, from war crimes to whoremongering, more and more editors will ask you to repeat your success. They will not be so thrilled to hear that you want to write about other topics. How you react to these pressures—for money, prestige, and professional credibility—will take a physical and emotional bite out of you. How will that affect your personal life? It could be tough.

I find that worrying about money and my editorial "image" are the biggest anti-aphrodisiacs ever. I don't get turned off because I've written too many erotic stories, but I do feel nonplussed when I find a shaky bank statement in my mailbox, or read a book review that rubs me wrong. I become very prickly when I feel threatened or resentful about my work, and that's the ultimate cold shower.

I don't like to write stories that I've written before. I don't like editors to tell me to dumb stuff down or to add gratuitous clichés. Some editors have hired me because they thought I'd write about all my one-night stands, and when we got to the end of the list they'd be done with me. They think of erotic writing as some kind of limited series of "true confessions." When I feel insulted by those kinds of offers and relationships, I honestly don't feel like fucking.

Not everyone is wired like this. I've got plenty of friends who soothe their frustrations by making love; it's the balm they need when they feel frustrated or blue. When I'm in a bad mood, however, sex isn't what I reach for. I've often wished it was—it would probably do me more good than chocolate, ill-advised shopping sprees, or watching television for hours with the blankets piled around my neck. But at least I've got my number.

The antidote for me is writing and editing as I please. Such creative freedom makes me a happy and sexually alert candidate. I never get sick of being turned on to a great new writer, and I never feel dull when I've written something I think is hot. When my writing is going well, both in quality and quantity, my sensual body is more willing to take a chance.

Is Sex Writing Killing Your Sex Life?

What if you honestly believe that your writing is messing with your libido? Let's take a closer look at your "condition."

- **Fresh Air and Filling Your Lungs**

Are you getting enough exercise? I'm convinced that the number-one sex killer in writers' lives is our lack of oxygen and physical movement. We spend entirely too much time slumped in a chair, at a keyboard. Our breathing is compromised for hours at a time; we're stiff and achy, popping painkillers for our miserable joints. I never dreamed when I started writing that I'd need an "exercise program" to be successful in my craft, but now I'd put it at the top of the list. If you start moving enthusiastically, breathing deeply and sweating profusely outside the bedroom, then you will feel a thousand times better as a lover and as a writer. This is one of those pieces of advice that has no exceptions. You just do it and it works.

- **Variety**

The next area to analyze would be the variety in your writing life. The answer to writing burnout isn't to stop writing—it's to stop writing the same old shit. Take the time to write letters, dreams, recipes, short stories, poetry, or country music lyrics. Instead of feeling more writers' fatigue when you hit your regular assignments, you'll feel relieved and even amused by your paycheck obligations.

- **Don't Cross Yourself**

A women's magazine once phoned me for an interview about how women could have better sex in an outdoor setting. I tried to think seriously about the subject, and I began, "Well, if she wants to have an orgasm—" But the editor cut me off: "No, no, we're not interested in that. Just tell us your advice if orgasm *isn't* the point!"

Not the point? I realized then that there was virtually nothing I could write for this magazine that wouldn't warp my brain. From my point of view, in any question about women's sex lives, those silly orgasms are always going to be at the heart of the matter.

There's nothing as gross as a story that appears in public, with your name on it, that you can't abide. You can tell yourself that it's disposable, that it will be forgotten in tomorrow's trash, but, in fact, reputations are made and lost on these kinds of impressions. Someone who reads that article might not hear your name again for five years, and yet be stuck with that negative impression.

Sex Jag Exposed

Most concerns about writers' "sex jag" are really coded inquiries about creative burnout. Blaming sex as the source of a writer's problem is a frivolous distraction from more weighty burdens that make writers feel helpless and burned out.

If abstinence, in the author's bed or at the author's desk, were such a great panacea, you'd hear the success stories. Instead, there's a silence that points at the most intractable culprits—fatigue, conformity, and reluctant submission. Next time someone wants to start a debate about sex writers' burnout, you should pull out your writing schedule—not your soiled sheets—and have a substantial conversation about the real difficulties that all authors share.

What Are You Waiting For?

Two years ago, I wrote a book about the power of sexual creativity and erotic expression called *Full Exposure*. It actually started out as a book for writers—I wanted to write a work for the new century called *100 Lovers*, about the whole history of twentieth-century erotica. I'd still like to do that book—or is it an encyclopedia?

Full Exposure ended up as a book that asked, "What is your sexual philosophy?—And what are you going to do about it?" But I didn't insist that my readers themselves should begin to write.

This book is different. I wrote this book because of all the times I ever admired writers and wanted to take them home, show them everything I know, and share all my favorite tricks and confessions. I've spoken as candidly to you about writing and publishing as I would if you were in my living room.

If you take my advice, you'll be prepared for the fact that a professional career in writing—writing erotica, no less—is a wild card. Sometimes it's exhilarating, sometimes devastating, often weirdly anticlimactic. If you do find an audience for your work, you can expect to influence your readers beyond all rational calculation.

On the other hand, personal practice in erotic writing will land one sure result: You will learn some remarkable things about yourself that you didn't know. Your writing is, without a doubt, going to improve; your erotic empathy, the way you see and touch people sexually, will increase tenfold. You will meet a tall, dark stranger—and a fair, chubby one as well. You'll meet them all; every erotic character will be accessible to you, because your erotic imagination will create them from scratch.

I really don't know why more people don't write about their lives and their sexuality as a matter of course. Is it because the consequences are relatively unknown? Is it that people know in their gut that it would change their lives, and they're frightened by that? Do they sense that they would start hoping for things that they can't have, or dreading other things that might overwhelm them?

Maybe writing seems like too much hard work. A lot of us have been brainwashed to believe that writing is grind.

I started this book like I've started every other—crushing my pillow over my head and saying, "I'll never get through this!" To confide in you about my "writing life" has been an experience as intimate as any sex scene I've ever composed.

Writing is a discipline that takes a leap of faith, a belief that stones can roll away. The surprise is that there does seem to be magic buried in the act of writing; to grasp it, you need only be determined to express yourself. Writing does make you feel alive; it does indeed make you ripe for the plucking. Your writing process is as soulfully erotic as anything you'll ever do, whether you write erotica or not. It doesn't leave you, it doesn't get old, and it resists any cynicism or betrayals. Each story you write is a blind date, it's true, but at its blinding best, it's irresistible. How can you not take the chance?

Part VIII

Appendix

How to Nominate Stories for *The Best American Erotica* Series

The Best American Erotica (B.A.E.) series is an annual collection of the best erotic short fiction of the past year. I founded the series with Macmillan in 1993; it was then continued by Simon & Schuster, which has published the series since 1994.

B.A.E. is by far the widest-read erotica anthology in the world. It's been an American best-seller in many years. Authors who appear in the series have felt, quite rightly, that their inclusion is a testimony to their superior work in the genre.

The edition comes out each February, with stories that were published originally in the previous twelve to eighteen months.

The content and style of *The Best American Erotica* is wide-ranging. The work might have been published in North America, in any book, periodical, or Web site. Short stories, novel excerpts, scripts, prose poems, and autobiographical essays have all been selections in the past. There's no "subject" that won't be considered. I'm more interested in how you tell the story than in what sex act you are interpreting.

If you believe you fit the criteria, or would like to nominate someone whose work does, you are welcome to submit a copy of the published story for consideration. Please do read at least two editions of *B.A.E.* from previous years to get an idea of the quality and range of the work.

Send a paper copy of the manuscript you'd like to nominate, or a photocopy of its most recent appearance in print. Send any copyright/publisher information or contributor biographical notes that you may have. Do NOT send E-mail, E-mail attachments, or disks.

Mail your submissions and/or nominations to:

Susie Bright
B.A.E. Nominations
P.O. Box 8377
Santa Cruz, CA 95061

Internet Resources for Erotic Authors

The following is a list of sites that offer up-to-date information for publishing and networking for erotic authors. I emphasize "up-to-date" because any list of print resources I could give you would be quickly outdated. The Internet is the best place to find out who is in business, active, and involved in erotic publishing.

CleanSheets
http://www.cleansheets.com
Erotic magazine updated every week, including poetry, fiction, art, information, and commentary.

The Femme Erotic Circle
http://www.femmerotic.com
A multisite portal and general sexuality resource that is pansexual, prosexual, and seeks to empower the sexual aspect of all people. Promotes sizable content-based sites that do the same, that are independently produced, and that conduct ethical and fair consumer practices. An extensive open listing database of other sexuality resources, both on-line and off-line.

Libidomag.com
http://www.libidomag.com
Libido magazine, one of the most original and influential erotica magazines in the United States, is now on-line, with its tremendous range and talent in erotic photography, fiction, and critical reviews.

Jane's Guide

http://www.janesguide.com

One-stop portal for all things sexual on the Web, from high-brow erotica to hard-core porn, with both links and reviews.

Erotic Readers Association Author Resources List

http://www.erotica-readers.com

Resources for publishing electronically—links of interest to anyone looking for an electronic publisher.

- Resources for Self-Publishing: links of interest to anyone wanting to self-publish E-books
- Resources for Authors of Erotic Fiction: links to sites that have specific info for the erotica writer
- General Writing Resources: on-line dictionaries, thesaurus, encyclopedia, and grammar tip sheets
- Copyright Issues: valuable information on copyright concerns

Kilgore Trout Erotic Author's Page

http://www.freezone.co.uk/rgirvan/erofic2.htm

This collection of links is devoted to writing and literary criticism sites that touch on the genre of erotic fiction, a form chosen by many acclaimed high-profile authors at some time in their careers. They include both names from mainstream and popular genre fiction—Henry Miller, Anaïs Nin, Robert Silverberg, Brian Aldiss, Philip Jose Farmer, Samuel R. Delany, Anne Rice, and Nicholson Baker—and a new generation of activists such as Alice Joanou, Gloria Brame, Pat Califia, and Susie Bright.

Nerve

http://www.nerve.com

A magazine of exceptional photographs and writing about sex and sexuality for both men and women.

Scarlet Letters

http://www.scarletletters.com

Erotica from a feminine perspective, updated weekly, at three sites: scarlet-letters.com, scarleteen.com, and femmerotic.com. Scarletletters.com and the *Journal of Femmerotica* publishes adult erotica and sexual material that both entertain and educate. Scarleteen.com furnishes young adults and teens with vital sexual education and information.

Susie Bright's Home Page
http://www.susiebright.com
Learn more about this book and try out some of my favorite erotic writing exercises. Erotic writing workshops calendar, and other classes. Read more about *The Best American Erotica* series, answer a survey about your erotic favorites, and check out my latest stories.

Credits

Beck, Marianna, from "C Is for Closet, Crevice and Colossus." Reprinted in *The Best American Erotica 1994*, ed. Susie Bright, New York: Simon & Schuster, 1994. First appeared in *Libido*, vol. 5, no. 4, Fall 1993.

Boxer, Debra, from "Innocence in Extremis." Reprinted in *The Best American Erotica 2000*, ed. Susie Bright, New York: Simon & Schuster, 2000. First appeared in *Nerve: Literate Smut*, eds. Genevieve Field and Rufus Griscom. New York: Broadway Books, 1998.

Bright, Susie, "An Illuminating History of Sex Writing in America." Adapted from the introduction to *The Best American Erotica 1993*, ed. Susie Bright, New York: Macmillan, 1993.

———, "The Erotic Reader's Bill of Rights." Adapted from the introduction to *The Best American Erotica 1994*, ed. Susie Bright, New York: Simon & Schuster, 1994.

———, from "Dan Quayle's Dick," *Sexwise*, San Francisco: Cleis Press, 1995.

———, "Femmechismo." Adapted from "Introduction," *Herotica*, ed. Susie Bright, San Francisco: Down There Press, 1988.

———, from *Full Exposure*, San Francisco: HarperSanFrancisco, 1999.

Butler, Mark, from "Cool, Clean, and Crisp." Reprinted in *The Best American Erotica 1994*, ed. Susie Bright, New York: Simon & Schuster, 1994. First appeared in *Paramour*, vol. 1, no. 1, Fall 1993.

Califia, Pat, from "Unsafe Sex." Reprinted in *The Best American Erotica 1994*, ed. Susie Bright, New York: Simon & Schuster, 1994. First appeared in *The Melting Point*, Boston: Alyson Publications, 1993.

Christina, Greta, from "Are We Having Sex Now or What?" *The Erotic Impulse*, ed. David Steinberg, Los Angeles: J. P. Tarcher, 1992.

Daly, Lloyd W., from *Aesop Without Morals*, New York: Thomas Yoseloff, 1961.

Hendriks, Vicki, from "ReBecca." Reprinted from *The Best American Erotica 2000*, ed. Susie Bright, New York: Simon & Schuster, 2000. First appeared in Nerve.com, 1998.

Jacobs, Alexandra, from "Enough! The Overexposure of Sex Is Ruining the Mood for Everyone," *New York Observer*, November 8, 1999.

Kamani, Ginu, from "Waxing the Thing." Reprinted in *The Best American Erotica 2001*, ed. Susie Bright, New York: Simon & Schuster, 2001. First appeared in *Junglee Girl*, San Francisco: Aunt Lute Press, 1995.

McCabe, Adam, from "The Maltese Dildo." Reprinted in *The Best American Erotica 2000*, ed. Susie Bright, New York: Simon & Schuster, 2000. First appeared in *Sex Toy Tales*, eds. Anne Semans and Cathy Winks, San Francisco: Down There Press, 1998.

Michaels, Magenta, from "Taking Him on a Sunday Afternoon." Reprinted in *The Best American Erotica 1993*, ed. Susie Bright, New York: Macmillan, 1993. First appeared in *Herotica 2*, ed. Susie Bright, New York: Plume, 1992.

Moore, Susanna, from *In the Cut*. Excerpt reprinted in *The Best American Erotica 1996*, ed. Susie Bright, Simon & Schuster, 1996. First appeared in *In the Cut*, New York: Random House, 1995.

Puzo, Mario, from *The Godfather*, New York: G. P. Putnam's Sons, 1969.

Schone, Robin, from "A Lady's Pleasure," from *Captivated*. New York: Kensington Publishing Corp., 1999.

St. Aubin, Susan, from "This Isn't About Love," from *Herotica 2*, ed. Susie Bright, New York: Plume, 1992.

Tea, Michelle, from "10 Seconds to Love," from *Starf*cker*, ed. Shar Rednour, Los Angeles: Alyson Publications, 2001.

Tourney, Anne, from "Full Metal Corset." Reprinted in *The Best American Erotica 1994*, ed. Susie Bright, New York: Simon & Schuster, 1994. First appeared in *Future Sex*, issue 3, 1993.

Willis, Danielle, from "Elegy for Andy Gibb." Reprinted in *The Best American Erotica 1994*, ed. Susie Bright, New York: Simon & Schuster, 1994. First appeared in *Dogs in Lingerie*, San Francisco: Zeitgeist Press, 1993.

You can find all these books hotlinked at http://www.susiebright.com

References

This is all simply by way of leading up to the general sexual
confusion which prevailed at this time. It was like taking a
flat in the Land of Fuck.
Henry Miller, *Tropic of Capricorn*

Aesop, ed., Bernard McTigue, ed. and trans., *The Medici Aesop: The Spencer Collection of the New York Public Library*, New York: Henry A. Abrams Publishers, 1989.

Anonymous, *A Man with a Maid*, New York: Blue Moon Books, reissue edition, 1996.

———, *The Pearl*, New York: Book-of-the-Month Club, 1996.

Arsan, Emmanuelle, *Emmanuelle*, New York: Grove Press, 1994.

Baker, Nicholson, *The Fermata*, New York: Vintage Books, 1995.

———, *Vox*, New York: Vintage Books, 1995.

Ballard, J. G., *Crash*, New York: Noonday Press, 1996.

Blank, Joani, ed., *I Am My Lover: Women Pleasure Themselves*, San Francisco: Down There Press, 1998.

———, *Femalia*, San Francisco: Down There Press, 1994.

Bright, Susie, *Susie Sexpert's Lesbian Sex World*, San Francisco: Cleis Press, 1998.

Bright, Susie, ed., *The Best American Erotica 1993*, New York: Macmillan, 1993.

———, *The Best American Erotica 1994*, New York: Simon & Schuster, 1994.

———, *The Best American Erotica 1995*, New York: Simon & Schuster, 1995.

———, *The Best American Erotica 1996*, New York: Simon & Schuster, 1996.

————, *The Best American Erotica 1997*, New York: Simon & Schuster, 1997.

————, *The Best American Erotica 1999*, New York: Simon & Schuster, 1999.

————, *The Best American Erotica 2000*, New York: Simon & Schuster, 2000.

————, *The Best American Erotica 2001*, New York: Simon & Schuster, 2001.

————, *Herotica*, San Francisco: Down There Press, 1988.

————, *Herotica 2*, New York: Plume, 1991.

————, *Herotica 3*, New York: Plume, 1994.

Brite, Poppy Z., *Lost Souls*, New York: Dell Publishing, 1993.

Bukowski, Charles, *Notes of a Dirty Old Man*, San Francisco: City Lights Books, 1981.

Burton, Sir Richard Francis, ed., *The Arabian Nights' Entertainments, or the Book of a Thousand Nights and a Night*, New York: Modern Library, 1997.

Bushnell, Candace, *Sex and the City*, New York: Warner Books, 1997.

Califia, Pat, *Doc and Fluff: The Dystopian Tale of a Girl and Her Biker*, Boston: Alyson Publications, 1996.

————, *Macho Sluts*, Boston: Alyson Publications, 1989.

————, *No Mercy*, Boston: Alyson Publications, 2000.

Califia, Pat, ed., *Doing It for Daddy*, Boston: Alyson Publications, 1994.

Casanova, Giacomo, *History of My Life, Vol. I–XII*, Baltimore: Johns Hopkins University Press, 1997.

Chin, Tsao Hsueh, *Dream of the Red Chamber*, Torrance, Calif.: Heian International Inc., 1996.

Corinne, Tee, *The Cunt Coloring Book*, San Francisco: Last Gasp Publishing, 1989.

Daly, Lloyd W., trans. and ed., *Aesop Without Morals*, New York: A. S. Barnes and Co., 1961.

De Sade, le Marquis, *Justine, Philosophy in the Bedroom and Other Writings*, New York: Grove Press, 1990.

Di Prima, Diane, *Memoirs of a Beatnik*, New York: Penguin USA, 1998.

Dodson, Betty, *Sex for One: The Joy of Self-Loving*, New York: Crown Publishing, 1996.

Dworkin, Andrea, *Intercourse*, New York: Free Press, 1997.

————, *Pornography: Men Possessing Women*, New York: E. P. Dutton, 1989.

Eighner, Lars, *Wank: The Tapes*, New York: Masquerade Books, 1998.

Ellis, Bret Easton, *American Psycho*, New York: Vintage Books, 2000.

Federation of Women's Health Centers, *New View of a Woman's Body*, Los Angeles: Feminist Health Press, 1991.

Fein, Ellen, and Sherrie Schneider, *The Rules: Time-Tested Secrets for Capturing the Heart of Mr. Right*, New York: Warner Books, 1996.

Ford, Mike, ed., *Once Upon a Time: Erotic Fairy Tales for Women*, New York: Masquerade Books, 1996.

Friday, Nancy, *Forbidden Flowers*, New York: Pocket Books, 1993.

———, *My Secret Garden*, New York: Pocket Books, 1998.

Galen, *The Sharp Edge of Love*, Portland, Oregon: Galen's Realm, 2000.

Ginsberg, Allen, *Howl and Other Poems*, San Francisco: City Lights Books, 1991.

Heinlein, Robert A., *Stranger in a Strange Land*, New York: Ace Books, 1995.

Hite, Shere, *The Hite Report: A Nationwide Study of Female Sexuality*, New York: Bookthrift Company, 1984.

Hollander, Xaviera, *The Happy Hooker*, Cutchoque, N.Y.: Buccaneer Books, 1996.

Holingshurst, Alan, *The Swimming Pool Library*, New York: Vintage Books, 1989.

Hoyland, Jon, and Joy Hoyland, eds., *Bad Sex*, New York: Serpents Tail, 1994.

Jaivin, Linda, *Rock 'N' Roll Babes from Outer Space*, New York: Broadway Books, 1999.

Jong, Erica, *Fear of Flying*, New York: Signet, 1996.

King, Woodie, and Ron Milner, eds., *Black Drama Anthology*, New York: Meridian Books, 1986.

Lawrence, D. H., *Lady Chatterley's Lover*, New York: Bantam Classics, 1983.

Lowenthal, Michael, ed., *Flesh and the Word 4: Gay Erotic Confessionals*, New York: Plume, 1997.

Mamet, David, *Oleanna*, New York: Vintage Books, 1993.

Miller, Henry, *Black Spring*, New York: Grove Press, 1989.

———, *Tropic of Cancer*, New York: Grove Press, 1989.

———, *Tropic of Capricorn*, New York: Grove Press, 1987.

Millett, Kate, *Sexual Politics*, Urbana, Ill.: University of Illinois Press, 2000.

Morin, Jack, *The Erotic Mind*, New York: Harperperennial Library, 1996.

Muscio, Inga, *Cunt*, Seattle: Seal Press, 1998.

Nin, Anaïs, *Delta of Venus*, New York: Pocket Books, 1990.

———, *Little Birds*, New York: Pocket Books, 1990.

Pond, Lily, ed., *Seven Hundred Kisses: A Yellow Silk Book of Erotic Writing*, San Francisco: HarperSanFrancisco, 1997.

Preston, John, *Mr. Benson*, New York: Masquerade Books, 1998.

Preston, John, ed., *Flesh and the Word 2: An Anthology of Erotic Writing*, New York: Plume, 1993.

———, *Flesh and the Word: An Anthology of Erotic Writing*, New York: Plume, 1992.

Preston, John, and Michael Lowenthal, eds., *Flesh and the Word 3: An Anthology of Gay Erotic Writing*, New York: Penguin USA, 1995.

Reage, Pauline, *The Story of O*, New York: Blue Moon Books, 1998.

Rechy, John, *City of Night*, New York: Grove Press, 1988.

Rednour, Shar, ed., *Starf*cker*, Los Angeles: Alyson Publications, 2001.

Rice, Anne (writing as A. N. Roquelaure), *Sleeping Beauty Trilogy*, New York: New American Library, 1999.

Roche, Thomas, *Noirotica 3: Stolen Kisses*, San Francisco: Black Books, 2000.

———, *Noirotica: An Anthology of Erotic Crime Stories*, New York: Masquerade Books, 1996.

———, *Pulp Fiction: Noirotica 2*, New York: Masquerade Books, 1997.

Rogers, Rosemary, *Sweet Savage Love*, New York: Romance Alive Audio, audio cassette version [book is out of print], 1995.

Rose, M. J., and Angela Adair-Hoy, *How to Publish and Promote Online*, New York: St. Martin's Press, 2001.

Samois, ed., *Coming to Power: Writings and Graphics on Lesbian S/M*, Boston: Alyson Publications, 1983.

Schone, Robin, *The Lady's Tutor*, New York: Kensington Publishing, 1999.

Semans, Anne, and Cathy Winks, eds., *Sex Toy Tales*, San Francisco: Down There Press, 1998.

Snitow, Ann, "Mass Market Romance: Pornography for Women Is Different," in *Powers of Desire*, Ann Snitow, Christine Stansell, and Sharon Thompson, eds., New York: Monthly Review Press, 1983.

Spillane, Mickey, *I, the Jury*, New York: Otto Penzler, 1996.

Steinberg, David, *The Erotic Impulse*, Los Angeles: J. P. Tarcher, 1992.

Steinberg, David, ed., *Erotic by Nature: A Celebration of Life, of Love, and of Our Wonderful Bodies*, San Francisco: Down There Press, 1988.

Susann, Jacqueline, *Valley of the Dolls*, New York: Grove Press, 1997.

Tan, Cecilia, *Black Feathers: Erotic Dreams*, New York: HarperCollins, 1998.

———, *Telepaths Don't Need Safe Words*, Cambridge, Mass.: Circlet Press, 1992.

Tea, Michelle, *The Passionate Mistakes and Intricate Corruption of One Girl in America*, Brooklyn, N.Y.: Semiotext, 1998.

Travis, Aaron, *Slaves of the Empire*, New York: Masquerade Books, 1998.

Tulchinsky, Karen, ed., *Hot and Bothered: Short Fiction of Lesbian Desire*, Vancouver: Arsenal Pulp Press, 1998.

Twain, Mark, *The Diaries of Adam and Eve: Translated by Mark Twain*, San Francisco: Fair Oaks Press, 1998.

Updike, John, *Couples*, New York: Random House, 1968.

Zipes, Jack, trans., *The Complete Fairy Tales of the Brothers Grimm*, New York: Bantam Books, 1992.

You can find all of these books hotlinked at http://www.susiebright.com

SUSIE BRIGHT is the founding editor of *The Best American Erotica* (1993 to the present), the *Herotica* series (volumes 1–3), and *On Our Backs* magazine (1984–1990). She is a prolific book author and journalist, the producer and host of the audio show "In Bed with Susie Bright" on Audible.com, and teaches erotic writing, film, and criticism worldwide. She lives in northern California with her partner and daughter. Her complete biography, résumé, and FAQ can be found at: http://www.susiebright.com.